# TEACHING
# IN THE NOW

# TEACHING IN THE NOW

## JOHN DEWEY ON THE EDUCATIONAL PRESENT

JEFF FRANK

Purdue University Press, West Lafayette, Indiana

Copyright 2019 by Purdue University. All rights reserved.
Printed in the United States of America.

Cataloging-in-Publication data is on file with the Library of Congress.
Paper ISBN: 978-1-55753-806-2
epub ISBN: 978-1-61249-590-3
epdf ISBN: 978-1-61249-591-0

# Contents

# Thinking With Dewey

This book is motivated by the belief that John Dewey's thinking continues to matter, and by a fear that Dewey's power to unsettle habituated modes of thinking and inspire creative responses to prevalent antidemocratic tendencies in our time has been greatly reduced, because—and despite Dewey's own warnings—it has been cast into a noun, Deweyan thought, instead of a verb, Dewey thinking. Dewey wants us to think *with* him, in our present moment. He does not want to be blindly accepted, let alone revered, and this book is intended to be a retrieval of the dynamism of Dewey's thinking for teaching and learning in our time.

Specifically, I worry that Dewey's wonderful little book *Experience and Education*, though widely assigned in teacher education and foundations of education courses and heavily cited in student papers and educational research literature, can come to be revered and not mobilized as something we can continue to think with as we make the attempt to address the problems that matter most to us, now, in our present moment. To put the point another way, I see my book as something like an invitation to think with Dewey again, or to think anew with Dewey. For students reading *Experience and Education* for the first time, I see this book as a companionable introduction, helping students see why Dewey's thinking continues to matter. For educators in schools of education, I hope this book—especially in the ways it uses generous selections from *Experience and Education* and Dewey's other writings on education—can help reanimate our appreciation of Dewey's thinking while suggesting new ways of making his work come alive for your students: future teachers, teacher educators, and lifelong students of education who will have a voice in the quality of the present our next generations experience.

As I will discuss in brief detail in the introduction, this book draws on Dewey scholarship and my own background as a philosopher of education, but the book's primary aim is not to contribute to philosophical discussions of Dewey. Rather, as someone with a background in philosophy of education but who is a teacher educator routinely teaching foundations courses and teacher education courses, I am most interested in highlighting some of the ways that Dewey's thinking can help us reanimate and reconstruct our lives as educators.[1] The tone will, at times, be personal, even impassioned. This is not because I aim to convince you that you should feel as I feel or think as I think. Instead, it is meant to remind us that Dewey's words can still move us to see our current work, and the world we live in now, anew. And, given the deep threats to democracy that seem to appear with each passing day, that ability to kindle democratic hope, if not create democratic practices, is something I am deeply grateful for.

It is in this spirit of gratitude that I welcome you to think with Dewey as you consider the educational problems that are on your mind and engage your attention and care. I call this work a pedagogical exercise, because I believe that the process of reading Dewey discloses new possibilities for democracy and education that make us better teachers and frees our students for growth that they may have never thought they were capable of.

# Waiting

For many the experience of schooling might be best summed up by the Rolling Stones' song "I am Waiting."[1] As Philip Jackson (1968/1990) strikingly demonstrates in *Life in Classrooms*, students spend much of their time in school waiting. They are quite literally waiting—waiting a turn, waiting for peers to complete work, waiting for the bell, waiting for the announcements to be over, and so on—but, equally important, the habit of waiting instilled and enforced in school forms character. Here is the way Jackson describes it:

> We have already seen that many features of classroom life call for patience, at best, and resignation, at worst. As he learns to live in school our student learns to subjugate his own desires to the will of the teacher and to subdue his own actions in the interest of the common good. He learns to be passive and to acquiesce to the network of rules, regulations, and routines in which he is embedded. He learns to tolerate petty frustrations and accept the plans and policies of higher authorities, even when their rationale is unexplained and their meaning unclear. Like the inhabitants of most other institutions, he learns how to shrug and say, "That's the way the ball bounces." (p. 36)

Though Jackson's work was originally published in 1968, as Martinez and McGrath (2014) argue, his analysis is sadly—but maybe not surprisingly given how powerful the grammar of schooling is (Tyack & Cuban, 1995)—still an accurate description of many schools in the United States. The type of *character* our schools create is one that we need to consider. Though explicit questions related to character education often get more attention,[2] Jackson's analysis remains important because these louder questions often hold us captive, keeping us from seeing that character is always already being taught in schools. In a classroom where students make their own rules and are given a great deal of trust to make their own choices, one form of character is taught; in a classroom that strongly adheres to zero tolerance discipline, quite a different form of character is taught. The very choices we make as teachers when it comes to the countless daily decisions we are called to make creates a culture in our class that helps form the character of the students in that class.[3] It is this hidden curriculum of character education that needs to be exposed and examined because it has a far greater influence than we think, often because we don't give it thought at all.[4]

For Jackson, the passivity taught in schools is antithetical to creative and intellectual work. Creative and intellectual work can be fostered in an environment of compliance, but is this the best we can do? The character of the creative person and the intellectual is often very different from the character of the individual resigned to the status quo. Schools that teach resignation and waiting aren't cultivating the character we claim to want in graduates. In addition, Debbie Meier (1995/2002) makes a strong and all too relevant (especially given the political climate surrounding America's 2016 election and renewed calls to arm teachers) connection between the hidden curriculum of schools and politics. It is a long quote, but worth considering in full:

> We see our schools as lawless Western towns, in need of a tall man in the saddle.
>
> But it's important to remember that even at best these heroes are usually charismatic bullies (it's not surprising that they're rarely women), and that they sometimes confuse "law and order" with a disrespect for any law besides themselves. They revel in their aloneness

and we are generally aware of an aura of violence that they bring with them. The violence of the young is quelled by counter-violence. The problem is not merely that there aren't enough such "leaders" to go around, but that these are not images of adulthood that encourage youngsters or teachers to use their minds well, to work collaboratively, or to respect the views of others. Models of such machismo have an impact. Their latent political consequences for a democratic society are dangerous. (pp. 127–128)

Although Richard Rorty (1998) is being heralded as prophetically announcing the election of Donald Trump, I see something similarly prescient in Meier's warning here.[5] If school puts the ends of compliance as paramount, then we get into a position where using our minds well, collaborating, and respecting others and their views—in short, living democratically—become subsumed to law and order, no excuses, zero tolerance, and other authoritarian-leaning policies. The threat to democracy and education becomes very real as these policies are lauded and enacted in schools, and yet we divert our attention away from the antidemocratic practices that are hidden in plain sight and to disputes that generate tremendous amounts of sound and fury—the Common Core being a major one[6]—and so we often don't turn our attention to the very real threat to democracy that is within our control as teachers to change. We need to focus on creating schools where democratic dispositions are cultivated, where children are appropriately challenged, and where authoritarianism in all its forms is called out and rooted out. Instead, we have wishful thinking: If only the Common Core were repealed, if only technology were used more (or less) in schools, if only we could fire teachers or pay teachers more, if only, if only. . . . It will be then, in that future, that everything will be okay. We keep waiting—for a cowboy, for a superhero, for the silver bullet (Kirp, 2015)—and this spirit of waiting can cause us to ignore and desecrate the great wells of democracy (Marble, 2003) just waiting to give us life, if we were willing to put in the work. Now.

But, we give ourselves over to waiting—and its related, if ordinary (Shklar, 1984), vices of nostalgia and ungrounded optimism or magical thinking—and lose the present. The goal of this book is to bring our attention back to the educational present, reminding us that we can take control of our educational present now; and that taking this control now is the only way to bring our desired future into being. Our classrooms, each day, are opportunities to exercise democracy or to excise it. The ways we interact with children and adolescents, the ways we provide feedback to students and solicit feedback from students, the ways we interact with colleagues: Though outside policies offer very real constraints on these, such constraints are not our fate. By setting democratic ideals and working toward them, we enact the future we want to see in our present interactions. This is certainly an ideal, but it isn't idealistic in the pejorative usage. Though Jackson's descriptions of school are complexly and fascinatingly true, to say that a better future is unrealistic—one where democracy is realized in every interaction—says more about our lack of will and creativity than it does about the state of nature or human potential. We are adaptable; given one environment we will more easily grow into fascists; given another, we will more easily grow into a living democracy. We don't find these environments written into the fabric of the world; we need to found them, building—through hard, collaborative, creative work—the conditions that will allow the future we desire to come into being.

The ideas expressed in the foregoing paragraph are certainly not new ones; they form the heart of John Dewey's thinking on democracy and education. To say they are not new is not to say that they've been tried and found wanting; rather, my goal in returning to them is two-fold. First, I aim to bring our attention to an aspect of John Dewey's educational thought that has not received the attention it deserves.[7] Surprisingly, Dewey has written about the importance of the present as it relates to education at every stage of his writing career,[8] and it forms—in many ways, and as I hope to demonstrate—key elements of his two most important works on education, *Democracy and Education* and *Experience and Education*. Yet very little has been written on the specifically educational importance of taking Dewey's thinking on the present seriously. I think it is a mistake not to focus on the importance of the present when we think about the significance of Dewey's educational thought, and a goal of this book is to discover what Dewey aims to teach us about education by focusing on the present. Second, I hope to make a compelling case that John Dewey's ideal of creating the fullest present moment as the only way to create the future we hope for is an ideal worth getting behind and working to realize in our present. I will make this case both through close readings of John Dewey's work and examples drawn from classrooms and lived experience. In the end, I hope making this argument will build our conceptual resources while also suggesting practices that are worth experimenting with and further developing.

To close, and as I suggest above, the stakes of not living democratically in the present are high; we need to stop waiting and hoping and begin the difficult process of building an educational present that will become the future embodied by our ideals.[9] We cannot wait to get our classrooms in order through traditional forms of discipline as a means to creating the democratic classroom we desire. We need to experiment with democracy right now as a means to deepening those nascent democratic practices in our future. We cannot wait for "the basics" to be covered before we can immerse ourselves in meaningful learning experiences: the best ground for meaningful learning experiences in the future is meaningful learning in the present. Again, this may seem pejoratively idealistic, but to assume so is to concede defeat prematurely. It takes creativity and work to realize our ideals in the present, and to write these ideals off as unrealistic before sufficient experimentation is not to be tough minded; to echo William James (1907/1998), it is to shirk our responsibility to the possible. As Langston Hughes (1951) provokes us to respond to the question "What happens to a dream deferred?" in his poem "Harlem," I think we can ask this question with similar troubling results in a poem called "School" with the same first line. What happens to all the deferring that takes place in schools? What becomes of our deference to what we take to be the "reality" of school as circumscribed by limited imaginations and lack of ideals? How much potential is squandered as we wait for the future that we imagine but aren't yet working to create? Dropout rates, school violence, lack of civic engagement don't even begin to tell the story of all this lost potential: we need to revive a hope that individuals, and our democracy, can be so much better—now—by creating a present, or working with others actively involved in creating a present, worthy of the name educative.[10]

## CHAPTER 1

# Opening Complexities

John Dewey (2008h) opens *Experience and Education* with this thought: "Mankind likes to think in terms of extreme opposites. It is given to formulating its beliefs in terms of *Either-Ors*, between which it recognizes no intermediate possibilities" (LW.13.5).[1] It is telling and important that in Dewey's final major work on education he begins by reminding us that mankind likes to think in opposites, but Dewey does not. Telling, because John Dewey has been vilified or praised for positions that he does not hold,[2] and important because though Dewey's thinking—or the idea of Dewey—may provoke strong reactions, Dewey aimed to invite thought beyond the simplistic dualistic categorizations we are all too apt to rely on and engage with when thinking. Thinking is difficult, and because Dewey's writing is meant to provoke thought that asks us to step outside of habituated modes of thinking, Dewey's work is difficult. I mention this at the outset, because it is important to know what we are getting into. We may have a vague sense of what Dewey is—progressive, liberal, anti-religion, instrumentalist, pragmatist—but these labels often say more about an unwillingness to think with Dewey than it does about what Dewey thinks. For this reason, I aim to offer what Philip Jackson (2002) calls "an appreciative exegesis" (p. 167) of John Dewey on the present: appreciative, because Dewey continues to remain relevant to education; exegetical, because his thought is often challenging to understand and needs interpretive work before it is seen to be as relevant as it is.

Reading appreciatively is not to claim that Dewey is infallible; but, it is to say that the present study will focus on one aspect of his thinking—the educational present—that I believe he gets right in a profoundly important way. This will be the focus of my work. My aim is to think with Dewey on the educational present, ignoring labels that often obscure more than they illuminate, sticking closely to his texts with an eye toward showing why we should take Dewey's thought as seriously as possible.

In addition to recognizing how complex Dewey's thought is because it goes against the grain of the labels we often want to attribute and affix to Dewey, there is a second difficulty. David Hawkins (2000) puts the point nicely: "It is not easy to criticize Dewey, because when you do you usually find that he has made the necessary qualifications somewhere else in his vast writings" (p. 109). Dewey's collected works are vast, and Dewey often rewrote sections of his major works when he realized he was mistaken. It is hard to criticize Dewey because closer readings of Dewey will generally show that Dewey anticipates and overcomes our objections. Because of this, there is a tendency to underappreciate Dewey's complexity in order to make—or score—a point.[3] As readers of Dewey, I think it is important that we hold off arguing against, or throwing our full support behind, Dewey and attempt to read Dewey closely, letting his writing expand the ways we think about education and our students.

Finally, Dewey always believed that good educational writing reconstructs the theory/practice divide. There is writing that is merely theoretical in education—that is, work that has next to nothing to do with the life of schools or classrooms—and there is writing that may be found immediately useful, but which doesn't offer grounds for thinking and continued growth as an educator. Dewey hoped to avoid both ends of this polarity, as do I. In particular, I want Dewey's thinking on the present to help teachers think about their classroom in new ways and creatively and critically engage with Dewey's thinking on the educational present to reconstruct the ways they teach and think about teaching. To do this, I aim to do justice to Dewey's thought, without becoming mired in scholarly details and debates that can prove distracting, while also making connections to classroom practices as I understand and experience them.

This approach, I acknowledge, can be frustrating to both parties: not enough scholarship for some, not enough definite direction and guidance for others. This is a risk worth taking, an experiment that Dewey enacted each time he wrote. And, I am inspired by the success of work in this vein from before Dewey and into the present. There are too many to mention them all, so I instead want to focus on one model that I find particularly worth aspiring to, and close to my own project. Carol Rodgers (2002) effectively reconstructs the theory practice dualism in her work on Dewey's vision of reflection. Rodgers offers an accurate and compelling reading of Dewey that wears its learning unobtrusively, and it also offers practicing teachers and teacher educators much to think about when it comes to Dewey and their own practices. Again, I could name others who do this work as well,[4] but highlight Rodgers (2002) because her ability to think with Dewey in a way that speaks very directly to the practice of teaching and teacher education is most like what I hope to accomplish here.[5]

This is just a brief snapshot of how I will approach the complexity of Dewey's thinking in this book. In the following sections of this chapter I begin discussing the complexities of certain themes that we will return to throughout the book.

## The Present: Finding a Way Between Quietism and Instrumentalism

One major motivation behind writing this book is a genuine and provocative puzzlement experienced in my classroom as we read books like *Democracy and Education* and *Experience and Education* and Dewey begins to address the purposes of schooling as it relates to a student's future. My students are, understandably so, concerned about their own futures, and they find it surprising that Dewey seems to downplay the importance of *preparing* for that future. Students who have just spent tremendous time, energy, and stress focused on preparing for the future of college that is now their present are not quite sure what to make of Dewey's assertion that the best preparation for the future is living in the fullness of the present. Beyond wondering what this might mean, there is the added feeling that Dewey can't be right; the feeling that there must be some importance, even some meaning, behind the drudgery they just endured in the name of preparing. Or else why—*why?*—would so many trusted adults insist upon the necessity of that preparation, an experience that often felt nothing like living in the fullness of the present?

Here is how Dewey (2008e) puts it in *Democracy and Education*:

> The mistake is not in attaching importance to preparation for future need, but in making it the mainspring of present effort. Because the need of preparation for a continually developing life is great, it is imperative that every energy should be bent to making the present experience as rich and significant as possible. Then as the present merges insensibly into the future, the future is taken care of. (MW.9.61)

In many ways, this quote is an excellent representation of how one might read Dewey closely so as to expand his significance for education. The formulation here is careful and precise, but it is also complex, and so lack of attention can lead a reader to walk away from this passage and into dualistic thinking. That is, we may read this passage and feel that Dewey is not interested—even against—preparing for the future. We can focus on the idea that "every energy should be bent to making the present experience as rich and significant as possible" and so conclude that Dewey is *against* preparing students for the future. But, this cannot be the case, because, "the need of preparation for a continually developing life is great." The picture is more complex than Dewey being *against* preparing for the future; he causes us to think about how the future can be "taken care of" by a life lived fully in the present.

Another way of getting at this complexity is to think about the instrumentalist dimensions of Dewey's thinking as weighed against what I would call the quietist side of living in the present. Dewey's instrumentalism can be briefly described as the idea that thinking is largely motivated by problems we confront in the world. When we find ourselves in a problem-situation, thought is activated to solve the problem. In this picture of thinking, we can see how inquiry is driven by, if not defined as, problem-solving. The use of thought is instrumental to the solving of problems.[6] To return to the example of my college students, getting to college is a problem that one uses thought to solve. The problem is getting into the best college; the solution is doing what it takes to get into that best college. Things like SAT tutoring, taking courses that one has little interest in but "look good," and doing "service work" are all *instrumental* to getting into the best college. Now, Dewey's picture cannot be this simplistic, but the fact remains that Dewey's thinking is geared toward bringing about a better—rather than a worse—future.

Saying this, thinking must be future-directed or oriented to the future, and this seems to fly in the face of what I am calling the quietist side of Dewey's thinking on the present.[7] That is, Dewey seems to imply that living fully in the present will be *the* preparation that one needs for the future. Being fully engrossed in a book, or a painting, or nature; losing time in the flow of conversation or inquiry;[8] experiencing wonder, awe, and love;[9] practicing mindfulness:[10] This is life lived meaningfully in the present. Living in the present is the centerpiece of many spiritual practices, and these practices are often explicitly unconcerned with what will happen in the future, leaving the future to a will that transcends the individual.

A compelling statement of this view can be found in Tolstoy's (1912/1997b) November 17th entry in his *Calendar of Wisdom*: "There is no past and no future; no one has ever entered those two imaginary kingdoms. There is only the present. Do not worry about the future, because there is no future. Live in the present and for the present, and if your present is good, then it is good forever" (p. 334).[11] In a very real way Tolstoy is correct—there is only the present, and so living fully in the present takes care of the future, because the future will only be our next present—but this type of stance can become problematic, because it may lead to a quietism that ignores the very real dangers of complacency and injustice. That is, if I am cultivating the fullness of my present, I can be insensitive to the reality that there may be a great deal of (white) privilege involved in this cultivation that can lead me to forget that *I* can live my spiritual practices because of *structural* injustices.[12] But, farmer and author Wendell Berry (2015) offers a useful counterpoint to this way of thinking when he notes: "maybe we could give up saving the world and start to live savingly in it" (p. 175). Here the thinking is—and this is a line of thought Tolstoy would endorse—we cannot stop injustice writ large, but we can practice justice in the relationships and interactions we live each day. Or, to put it in slogan form: Don't worry about the fate of mankind—something we cannot control—worry about the present you are living!

Dewey is complexly somewhere in the middle of all of this with his thinking on the present. Though Dewey has the intellectual humility to know the limitations of how an individual's thought and action can shape the future, he believes we must try to bring about the future we envision. It is through human will, thinking, and effort that we bring about our desired future, and thus we have an obligation to *create* the future we hope for. At the same time, mere instrumentalism—sacrificing the quality of our present experience for a distant future—is equally misguided. Here a reader may wonder: Isn't it clear that Dewey wants it both ways? And, I think the only answer is: Yes. Dewey wants us to live savingly in the present, but he also wants to save the future.

These stances aren't mutually exclusive, but it is extraordinarily difficult to have it both ways, despite Dewey's assertion that "as the present merges insensibly into the future, the future is taken care of." We create democracy by living democratically in the present; we create meaningful learning experiences by giving students meaningful work in the present; we prepare a student for the intellectual work demanded in college by having students do intellectually demanding work in the present.[13] These can all be stated clearly, but I want to be clear that these are ideals that take will, creativity, and intelligence to enact. In the following chapters I will show how this can happen; for present purposes, I want to give a brief overview of this complexity so that we can be mindful of it as we begin engaging in a more sustained way with Dewey's thinking on the educational present.

## Orientation to an Open Future

Another important complexity to be mindful of is Dewey's thinking about the openness of the future. Dewey was of the mind that preparation for the future was often fruitless because the future we are preparing for is in the process of being created. If we prepare for the future based on our experience of the past, we may be preparing for a world that doesn't exist.[14] Here is how Dewey puts the point (2008g) in a book review:

> There are many points of view from which the Victorian age may be regarded, and as many corresponding definitions of its essence. One of these definitions, at least as true as the others, is that it regarded the present as the culmination, the apogee, of the past. Hence its complacency. Today we think of the present as the preparation for a future; hence our disturbed uncertainty. (LW.6.280)

There are two dangers in this passage: complacency and "disturbed uncertainty." We know that the world is changing quickly. In the past, many could prepare for a job that was destined for them, through family connection or social station, and could rest complacent knowing that they didn't have to do much other than follow the path laid down and trod before them to live successfully. Now, this certainty—for what seems like a growing number of people—no longer exists. Importantly, it is very easy to move from disturbed uncertainty about the future to something like militant nostalgia. I think we can see this very clearly in things like the Brexit decision and the 2016 Presidential election in the United States. Instead of working with the reality of our changing world, very large numbers of people believe that we can, and should, return to an imagined world where there was more certainty and security (at least for white men).[15] Instead of being open to our changing present and using intelligence to build a desired future from this present, nostalgia reigns.

Here, again, is a tension and a place where Dewey's ideals and beliefs are very clear. Dewey was not afraid of change and he saw it as natural and something that should be worked with and shaped to our ideals. Dewey was anything but nostalgic; this doesn't mean, of course, that he is irreverent or aims to destroy things people value for the sake of destruction.[16] But, he does believe that things only get stronger the more responsive they are to the reality of change and growth. This very idea—as seen by the bitter dismissal of Dewey by some conservative and conservative Christian critics[17]—can feel threatening, but I don't think this needs to be the case.

Though Dewey's views may seem to be more suited to liberal nonbelievers, I think it is far more inclusive and interesting than that. Dewey is interested in bringing about the best possible lives for the greatest number of people, and he invited the opportunity to work with anyone who shared this vision, regardless of their positionality. Dewey was not an ideologue, and we see this quite clearly in *Experience and Education*, where Dewey criticizes some of the very educational movements—variously described as progressive, or student-centered, or just "new"—that he is credited with inspiring. While Dewey believes that these new forms of education are generally responding to the right types of problems found in traditional approaches to education, their solutions to these problems often miss the mark and so stand in need of reconstruction.[18] Something with the label progressive isn't necessarily good, just as something labeled traditional or conservative isn't automatically bad. This is the type of either/or thinking Dewey's writing helps us see through.

To return to the importance of preparing for the reality of an open future, I turn our attention to a rather long quote written toward the end of Dewey's life and unpublished until his collected works were compiled. In this passage that is absolutely germane to our discussion, Dewey (2008i) muses:

The problem of so educating youth that they will be effective creators of the future—for it is only through creative acts that they can be its guardians—is a tremendously difficult one. The one certain thing about the future is its uncertainty, just as the only thing which is constant is change . . . The best possible preparation for any future is the development of certain attitudes in the present. When change is as rapid and as extensive as it now is, this applies with double force. What is wanted in the way of preparation for the future is that the young be so educated and aware that they are living in a world of change and realization that continued change is inevitable . . . Possession of an open mind is a necessary part of the disposition that can deal effectively with change; but too much of traditional education, especially in the school and other set forms of instruction, tends to create the closed mind—and the closed mind is that which is shut to realization of change and cannot cope with it. . . . There will be almost a revolution in school education when study and learning are treated not as acquisition of what others know but as development of capital to be invested in eager alertness in observing and judging the conditions under which one lives. Yet until this happens, we shall be ill-prepared to deal with a world whose outstanding trait is change. (LW.17.462–463)

I draw our attention to this passage because it emphasizes what is a key point we need to be mindful of when thinking about Dewey on living in the present as preparation. Dewey opens the quote with a beautiful reflection on the idea that the young become guardians of what is valuable—the conservative impulse he fully endorses—through *creation*. If we value sacred spaces, we need to create these spaces: what worked for the medieval European Christian can serve as inspiration, but it cannot be neatly replicated in our present.[19]

To prepare for the future we are called on to create, we cannot indulge in nostalgia or expect that the path to the future will be predictable. Instead, we are called to be the type of person who can deal effectively with change—who, indeed, invites it with an open mind—and who thinks creatively about how to best enact one's evolving values in an evolving world. This is a terribly difficult and complex thing to do, and we will consider what educators can do, now, to prepare students for this work in the following chapters; but, the point to keep in mind now is that <u>living in the fullness of the present</u> does not mean that one does <u>not have an orientation to the future</u>. One has a deep desire to build the best possible future, and one knows that this will only happen through a full acknowledgment of the reality of change and an openness to the changes that will inevitably occur in the future.[20]

## Childhood as Golden Impossibility

The title of this section is drawn from Emerson's (1844/1983b) essay "Experience," where he labels humanity a golden impossibility. What he means by this, amongst other things, is that it is impossible to circumscribe, or discover the limits of, human potential. This is something we need to be especially mindful of when we think about the *present powers* of children. Gareth Matthews (1996) makes the compelling case that developmental psychology can do more harm than good when the findings from psychological research, which are meant to be provide a parent and teacher with a sense for developmental milestones, are taken to be the fate of what a child can and cannot do in the present moment. While it is undoubtedly important to use the best psychology and the learning sciences to inform the practice of teaching, a paltry empiricism (again, to echo Emerson[21]) that doesn't allow for the freeing of potential must be disavowed.

Here is where it is important to keep in mind another tension in Dewey's thought. Dewey (2008f) was keenly interested in creating a science of education.[22] He believed that there was a tremendous amount of—what he calls—waste in education because the insights and practices of exceptional teachers often live and die with them: they aren't converted into a common resource that the greatest number of teachers can learn from. This is what Dewey meant by science in the context of education; he wanted what we now call best practices to become the common inheritance of teachers. So, Dewey would be heartened by developments in, for example, educational psychology and the learning sciences, because these promise to contribute to *what we know* about children and how to best educate them.[23] But, he would be very wary—as was William James (1899/1992)—about overpromising and promoting faddish applications of science over and against what teachers learn by working with children.

An interesting way of looking at this is to think about Hearne's (1986) work on the tensions between what animal trainers know and what scientists who study animals know.[24] Hearne makes the case that science often writes off as impossible: that a working German Shepherd knows things about situations that humans don't and can communicate this knowledge to a trusted human companion—what dog trainers know to be the case. Dewey would never want this to happen. For example, when someone like long-time early childhood educator and writer Vivian Paley tells us something about children that may contradict something found out about children in a more controlled environment, it is worth revising our theories developed in those environments and not distrusting Paley.[25] Or, when we see what children are capable of in, for example, a setting like a Danish forest school,[26] it is worth using this experience to push at the limits of the possible. For Dewey, a science of education should be expansive: it should inspire us to grow from the best of what we know into better futures.

Dewey reminds us across his writing on education that we need to appreciatively understand children and childhood. We mustn't fit expansive experience into theories we have about childhood, or see children as deficient forms of adulthood; rather, childhood has its own beauty, its own intelligence, its own grace that children grow from, through and into adulthood.[27] Dewey (2008c) puts it this way in *School and Society*:

> Life is the great thing after all; the life of the child at its time and in its
> measure, no less than the life of the adult. Strange would it be, indeed,
> if intelligent and serious attention to what the child *now* needs and is

capable of in the way of a rich, valuable, and expanded life should somehow conflict with the needs and possibilities of later, adult life. "Let us live with our children" certainly means, first of all, that our children shall live—not that they shall be hampered and stunted by being forced into all kinds of conditions, the most remote consideration of which is relevancy to the present life of the child. If we seek the kingdom of heaven, educationally, all other things shall be added unto us—which, being interpreted, is that if we identify ourselves with the real instincts and needs of childhood, and ask only after its fullest assertion and growth, the discipline and information and culture of adult life shall all come in their due season. (MW.1.37)

Dewey is expressing a pragmatic hope, or faith, in this quotation that is worth dwelling with.[28]

Listen again: "Strange would it be, indeed, if intelligent and serious attention to what the child *now* needs and is capable of in the way of a rich, valuable, and expanded life should somehow conflict with the needs and possibilities of later, adult life." Creating what a child needs *now* in the fullness of the present moment; it would be strange indeed if this somehow fails her or him as s/he grows and develops. This is not to say that it is easy to discern what a child needs and is capable of; this is not to say that it is easy to respond effectively to those needs and capacities; but, it is to say that we can attempt to create the educational equivalent of the kingdom of heaven for children now, given everything we know about and hope for children and childhood.

Shutting children indoors so they can do test preparation that will prepare them for further test preparation will equip them well indeed for a certain type of adult life. But, we have to think about the quality of that adult life, and the qualitative experiences of childhood that will lead to better—richer, more meaningful, more interesting, more engaged—futures. Here we approach the heart of Dewey's faith and hope: The best present experience is the only way to build a foundation for better experiences in the future. Putting aside questions of whether the present experience is enriching or interesting is a mistake that we succumb to often without giving it the thought it deserves. That is, how often do we subject students to numbing, constricting, humiliating (to use only a few adjectives) experiences in school—experiences that many of us may never want to re-live[29]—and yet manage to justify these experiences as preparatory, or at least necessary. But, we must also somehow know that Dewey is right: "Life is the great thing after all." When we watch children joyously experience life in a forest school, when we see children being treated with the respect and care of an educator like Paley, we can see a future worth living and creating. And, we gain perspective on just how limited and limiting education becomes when we look past the quality of the present as we try to justify under-educative experiences as preparatory for a future we are not actively envisioning as one worth living and creating.

This will be the focus of the next chapter: the *quality* of the present experience as the best preparation for a more expansive and educative future.

CHAPTER 2

# The Future Depends on the Quality of the Present

It is surprising that less attention has been paid to Dewey's thinking on the educational present, because once we start looking at his educational work through this lens, we begin seeing references to the present everywhere. Most significantly, when we go back to *Experience and Education* we see that the present is the linchpin to understanding the transition from old forms of education to new forms of education waiting to be developed.[1] Under traditional modes of education, the quality of a student's present experience was deemed less important than the future the student was preparing for. Progressive approaches to education were promising because they saw that the student's present experience shouldn't be neglected in favor of future experience.[2] But it needs to be kept in mind that Dewey was critical of progressive education. It is not the case that focusing on a child's enjoyment of the present moment or failing to think about the child's future was any better—in fact, it is often much worse—than the drive to prepare students for future success. Dewey (2008h) puts it this way in *Experience and Education*:

> Here, again, the problem for the progressive educator is more difficult than for the teacher in the traditional school. The latter had

indeed to look ahead. But unless his personality and enthusiasm took him beyond the limits that hedged in the traditional school, he could content himself with thinking of the next examination period or the promotion to the next class. He could envisage the future in terms of factors that lay within the requirements of the school system as that conventionally existed. There is incumbent upon the teacher who links education and actual experience together a more serious and a harder business. (LW.13.50)

The education that Dewey calls us to enact is certainly not lax; it is "a more serious and a harder business" than traditional education. Within the context of his thinking on the present, the traditional educator "could content himself with thinking of the next examination period or the promotion to the next class." It is not the job of the traditional educator to question the aims set by the system she finds herself in; her job is to make her students successful within this system.

If successful promotion to the next grade requires a score of eighty or above on an exit examination, then her main responsibility is to make sure her students score eighty or above. How the students get to eighty, or what happens after they reach eighty is not the central concern: The concern is the score and teaching so that students reach that score. Now, there is something extremely useful about this very clear focus and something admirable about a teacher taking responsibility for helping students meet this goal. In many ways, the resurgent interest in "no excuses" pedagogies demonstrates why traditional education might be preferable to more experimental methods.[3] But, Dewey wants us to think beyond the dualism of either "no excuses" or "no preparation/no hope for college." Though a progressive education may fail to prepare students for college, this doesn't have to be the case. More, downplaying, if not ignoring, the *quality* of a student's present experience may indeed be necessary in a "no excuses" style of teaching, but it is not the case that accounting for the *quality* of a student's experience will necessarily lead to an education that fails to prepare students for the future.[4]

We can have it both ways, but to do this is no easy feat; as Dewey warns us, "the problem for the progressive educator is more difficult than for the teacher in the traditional school." I want this to be very clear from the outset: Traditional education has merits, and any education worthy of the name must, at the very least, accomplish what traditional education allows students to accomplish, which is successful advancement in the social-educational system as it currently stands. A student educated in a progressive context should be able to attend college and excel once in college; this same student should be as prepared to land a job and do well in that job as her traditionally educated counterpart. But, succeeding in the system as it currently stands cannot be the only goal. As discussed in the previous chapter, the world is progressing at a rapid rate, and students need to be prepared for the changing world. More, the system as it currently stands is not an ideal one for many reasons, and so an education worthy of the name must also prepare students for more than succeeding in the world as it stands; they must also be prepared to improve the social-educational world they inherit and make their own.[5]

To begin understanding what this new education might look like, we need to focus our attention on what a *quality* educational experience is and looks like. Interestingly, this is something Dewey was thinking about very early in his career, before he published his major educational works. In an early essay on ethics titled "Self-Realization as Moral Ideal," Dewey (2008b) makes a point that could be found, in a more developed form, in *Democracy and Education* or *Experience and Education*. He writes:

> We have to a considerable extent, given up thinking of this life as merely a preparation for another life. Very largely, however, we think of some parts of this life as merely preparatory to other later stages of it. It is so very largely as to the process of education; and if I were asked to name the most needed of all reforms in the spirit of education, I should say: "Cease conceiving of education as mere preparation for later life, and make of it the full meaning of the present life" . . . An activity which does not have worth enough to be

carried on for its own sake cannot be very effective as a preparation
for something else. (EW.4.49–50)

As a sort of tangential line of thought in an essay on ethics, it
harbors thoughts that become central to Dewey's mature philosophy
of education. To start, Dewey draws an interesting comparison to a
religious belief in the afterlife and traditional education.

According to Dewey, we've given up thinking of life as a preparation for another life, but we've held onto the idea that education should
have a spirit of self-sacrifice and faith that suffering will ultimately
pay off. As a sociological point people may continue to believe in an
afterlife, but as a practical matter, Dewey sees his generation choosing
a quality present life over self-sacrifice in the here and now for divine
reward in the hereafter. One place we see this in stark detail is in our
thinking on schools. While many adults will say a certain amount of
externally imposed self-discipline and self-sacrifice is good for children,
if given the choice, many adults would not choose to trade the freedom
they have in adulthood for the forced compliance and drudgery found
in too many schools. Self-sacrifice and waiting for the future is fine
when you are a child, so goes this reasoning, but it is not something
that should be expected of adults. It is worth sitting with the point, and
seeing that Dewey believes that "the most needed of all reforms in the
spirt of education" is to stop conceiving of education as *mere* preparation and instead making it the full meaning of present life. And, it is
worth considering what Dewey means when he writes that an "activity
which does not have worth enough to be carried on for its own sake
cannot be very effective as a preparation for something else."

Here is where it is easy to think that Dewey is against "discipline" or
for teaching students to shirk hard work in favor of experiences that are
immediately agreeable. But, this is not the case at all. An experience can
still be difficult and yet also be fully engrossing of the present attention
of a child. One need only think about how seriously children take play
(Paley, 2005; Stilling, 2006) or how much dedication one can call forth
from a child when she is doing something—playing an instrument,
hiking a mountain, performing an experiment she cares about[6]—to

know that a child can be deeply invested—now, in the present—in something that is difficult.

More, when we think about those times when we don't have to demand a child's dedication and interest, we should think with Dewey: Are these moments that aren't explicitly about preparing for the future doing a child harm? Or, is it in these moments that the child is most learning habits of mind and heart that will serve her in whatever she does later in life? Do we need to force compliance through *mere* preparation in order to set a child on the course to deeper and more meaningful learning in the future? Or, isn't it worth breaking with, or fundamentally reconstructing, traditional education in order to achieve *both* full engagement and the type of learning that will set in place habits that will serve students most effectively in the future?[7]

If we return to another early essay by Dewey, we can see that it is the case that study of the traditional liberal arts is most certainly not precluded. If we believe in the liberal arts, we believe in them not because they are comprised of certain books; we believe in the liberal arts because of the type of person they lead us to become.[8] When we engage with important texts, we do so not merely because they are important texts, but because they are the types of text that elicit thought and cause us to grow in ways that other texts simply cannot promote in the same manner. Here is the way Dewey (2008a) puts it in an early essay about the college curriculum:

> The kingdom of heaven, in learning as in other matters, cometh not with observation. The general effects, the internal results, those which give the set and fix the attitude of the spirit, are the real effects of the college education. The average graduate may have no ready answer to the inquiry five years after his graduation, what use he now makes of all his learning, of his Greek, his Mathematics, his Old High German and his knowledge of Kant's *Critiques*. If he is wise, his thoughts will take somewhat this form: "All this is a matter of no account. The thing of importance is whether I have my interests trained to alert action and ready and wide vibration. Am I avoiding stagnation, both the apparent stagnation of mental idleness, and that

stagnation which simulates the form of action but is the mere vacant repetition and imitation of the thoughts of others? Above all, are my sympathies with whatever touches humanity, nearly or remotely, broad and dominant? If so, the Philistine may return to Gath; my college course has fulfilled its purpose, I have the *unum necessarium*—the one thing needful." (EW.3.54–55)

It is interesting that Dewey uses the language "kingdom of heaven" here as he does in *School and Society.*[9] Like Tolstoy (1883/1997a) in his *Gospel in Brief,* Dewey is interested in what it might mean to realize the kingdom of heaven in the present. And though Dewey has been accused of using the language of religion parasitically (Baurain, 2011), I think Dewey's fervor and devotion to drawing out the underexplored potential of education is accurately discussed using *religious* language.[10]

One studies to have one's spirit altered and made more expansive. This is what stands out in this early essay; the idea that education has transformative power, and the goal of education is not preparation in a narrow sense. As Dewey reminds us,

> The thing of importance is whether I have my interests trained to alert action and ready and wide vibration. Am I avoiding stagnation, both the apparent stagnation of mental idleness, and that stagnation which simulates the form of action but is the mere vacant repetition and imitation of the thoughts of others? Above all, are my sympathies with whatever touches humanity, nearly or remotely, broad and dominant?

This is what education should do for us; it should train the interests to ready and wide vibration, it should keep us from stagnation, it should help us avoid imitation, and it should make our sympathies alert, ready, and wide.

Dewey's thought develops from this early essay because he begins to more fully appreciate the importance of the present. Dewey will grow less sympathetic to the idea that "the average graduate may have no ready answer to the inquiry five years after his graduation, what use he now makes of all his learning." Less sympathetic, because Dewey will realize that a student's present interest must be accounted for, and teachers must be able to articulate the present value, even if nascent, behind the work they are doing with students. If our goal as educators is to keep the mind from stagnation and develop broad and engaged sympathies, we must begin that work now, and give students a more direct intimation of the possibilities of spirit that they are just beginning to cultivate through their studies. Waiting for students to appreciate education five years after graduation is a recipe for indifference, noncompletion of school, compliance, waste of potential: these and all the dangers discussed in the introduction. So, while Dewey will still hold to the spiritual value of a liberal arts education, he will want to see those values enacted and appreciated in the present, not made a promissory note *only* enjoyed with the accrual of time. Though some of the values will need time to fully develop, we must give students experience with these values and why they matter now, or risk tremendous waste of potential: the potential of individuals and the collective potential of the experiment in democracy and democratic education that is the United States.

## What Is an Educative Experience?

In *Experience and Education*, Dewey was interested in determining which types of experience were educative. He was of the mind that traditional forms of education—in neglecting the *quality* of an educational experience for fear of not preparing students—need reconstruction. But, he was also of the mind that *mere* experiential education was not enough, because not every experience is educative. Simply having an enjoyable or engaging experience does not mean that the experience is educative;[11] worse, these experiences are often mis-educative, rooting in place habits of mind that lead a student to become a person with narrowed sympathies and a weakened capacity for future growth. As such, mere experiential education is no substitute for mere preparatory education: We need to discover the meaning of an educative experience so that we can create an education for students worthy of the name.

Moving from one end of the polarity, mere preparation, to the other, mere enjoyment of experience, is mis-educative and the type of thinking Dewey warns us—from the beginning of *Experience and Education* and across his work—to avoid. When we think about the role of experience in education, Dewey (2008h) notes:

> The belief that all genuine education comes about through experience does not mean that all experiences are genuinely or equally educative. Experience and education cannot be directly equated to each other. For some experiences are mis-educative. Any experience is mis-educative that has the effect of arresting or distorting the growth of further experience. An experience may be such as to engender callousness; it may produce lack of sensitivity and of responsiveness. Then the possibilities of having richer experience in the future are restricted. Again, a given experience may increase a person's automatic skill in a particular direction and yet tend to land him in a groove or rut; the effect again is to narrow the field of further experience. An experience may be immediately enjoyable and yet promote the formation of a slack and careless attitude; this attitude then operates to modify the quality of subsequent experiences so as to prevent a person from getting out of them what they have to give. (LW.13.11–12)

Here we see Dewey very clearly aiming his criticism at experiential education when this education sees any experience as educative or preferable to traditional forms of education. As Dewey shows, this cannot possibly be the case, because there are many types of experience that aren't educative at all: In fact, they are mis-educative. So, even though we might agree that having a student prepare for a standardized test is not an educational ideal worth striving toward—following Dewey's own line of thinking—this preparation may often be preferable to *mere* experiential education as promoted by schools that call themselves progressive.[12] At least students preparing for a standardized test are learning information that may be of value; leaving students to find meaning in experience without mindfulness on the part of an educator often teaches nothing and can become counterproductive.

In the quote above—and across *Experience and Education*—the main criterion for the judging whether or not an experience is educative is the effect it has on future experience. If an experience makes growth in the future more likely or more expansive, it is educative; if it makes growth less likely or if it arrests growth, then the experience should not be considered educative. Growth is a central term in Dewey's philosophy of education, so it is worth discussing this directly before looking more closely at the quotation above.[13] Dewey's thinking on growth is meant to contrast with an education that is fitting students for some predetermined end. Vocational education that leads to a definite career in a trade, an academic track that leads to college and one of the professions: These are contrasted with education that is for growth. An education for growth means developing capacities and capabilities that can be mobilized to meet an ever-evolving present. Students learn how to learn in the process of addressing meaningful problems. The result of learning how to resolve and effectively respond to these types of problems leads the student to grow in her capacities and capabilities to address problems in the future. Learning to respond well to the problems that will inevitable arise over the course of our lives is, as will be discussed in more detail below, an education centered on growth. Education is not in the service of some predetermined end, a job or an honor, but is synonymous with the process of learning how to become more effective in meeting the problems we will inevitably face. Learning to more effectively respond to meaningful problems leads to growth, just as growth allows us to more effectively learn from our experiences.

Turning back to the examples from the quotation above, Dewey mentions that an experience can engender callousness, and this will produce lack of sensitivity and responsiveness in the future. What might this look like? One example from progressive education narrowly conceived is the introduction of a multicultural curriculum that highlights "multicultural heroes" or "multicultural holidays" without giving students a sense for structural racism or systemic injustices.[14]

Students who have "an experience" with multicultural education—they read about Rosa Parks, or celebrate Kwanza in the classroom—aren't necessarily having an educative experience. Some students may go away from this experience thinking they now know enough about others to act *knowingly* about others,[15] or feel as if nothing more needs to be done about injustices, because we now have holidays and we can just wait for the next hero to right any social wrong. This type of multicultural education, though often motivated by very good intentions, is mis-educative because it often leads to a type of callousness that does not promote a student's desire to learn more or engage more fully with the world.

We can see similar things happening with other experiences. Simply taking children to a museum or on a field trip does not mean that children are having an *educative* experience. Unless the trip to the museum makes the child want to learn more about art or engage in making art and prepare her to do both—how often is the highlight of the trip the experience with commercialism as we exit through the gift shop?—then despite the attempt at *experiential* education, these students might have learned just as much if not more by experiencing a traditional lecture on art and artists. Simply having an experience that isn't a "traditional" one doesn't ensure that learning happens.[16]

In addition, Dewey develops another example of how education in the present fails to prepare for a fuller future, because "a given experience may increase a person's automatic skill in a particular direction and yet tend to land him in a groove or rut; the effect again is to narrow the field of further experience." Here we see a more direct criticism of a staple of traditional education: the drill. A child repeats a performance over and over until it becomes automatic. Now, in some cases, this type of repetition might be necessary. We practice multiplication until it becomes second nature to us, thereby enabling us to do more complicated math with ease in the future. We are not stuck in a groove or rut; we are empowered to do wider more meaningful work in the future. But, for every case where this type of practice is empowering, there are counterexamples; the key is knowing the difference and acting on it.[17] For example, the scientific method is often taught formulai cally—as steps that one mechanically follows—and so students fail to *experience* the scientific method. Their further experience with science is narrowed, because the scientific method isn't taught in its engaging complexity: It is a worksheet with neat inputs and clear outcomes (Lee & Butler, 2003).

We can think of other examples. A coach who drills performances that are needed in games without giving athletes enough approxima- tions of game situations will ultimately underprepare athletes. Again, the drills have a place, but they cannot be applied mechanically, because in a game situation complexity often reigns. Too often, according to Dewey, we aren't thoughtful enough about the future and what it calls for. While a certain amount of drilling might be necessary, it is certainly not sufficient as preparation, and very often we can learn everything of value we need to learn when we approximate—as closely as possi- ble—the future tasks we are *merely* preparing to do now.[18]

Finally, Dewey admonishes us to consider that "an experience may be immediately enjoyable and yet promote the formation of a slack and careless attitude; this attitude then operates to modify the quality of subsequent experiences so as to prevent a person from getting out of them what they have to give." Here again we can see Dewey leveling his criticism at progressive approaches to education. Simply because a child enjoys an experience, or chooses an educational option thereby giving the impression of self-directed learning, it does not mean that the child is having an *educative* experience. In order for an experience to be edu- cative, it must offer the promise of a more *expansive* future. If the child must have fun in order to learn, then we can easily see that the child will not be prepared when learning gets complicated and challenging. In fact, as Carol Dweck (2006) has demonstrated, a learner's interest in facing challenges is far more predictive of persistence and long-term gains in learning than when a learner chooses ease. So, Dewey would be highly critical of activity for the sake of activity—as often happens in watered-down versions of constructivist pedagogy or differentiated instruction[19]—and would qualify the *quality* of an experience with the

ιonition that a quality educational experience is one that
*allenging* for students, thereby developing a mindset, in
eks out challenges in the future.

. clear, merely having an experience—even if it is an
enjoyable one—does not guarantee that the experience is an educative
one, and—as we've seen—a merely enjoyable experience often sets in
place habits that constrict and limit educational opportunities in the
future. These experiences must be avoided and certainly must not be
touted as better than traditional ways of educating. As a way of sum-
marizing this line of thought, Dewey (2008h) writes:

> Everything depends upon the *quality* of the experience which is had.
> The quality of any experience has two aspects. There is an imme-
> diate aspect of agreeableness or disagreeableness, and there is its
> influence upon later experiences. The first is obvious and easy to
> judge. The *effect* of an experience is not borne on its face. It sets a
> problem to the educator. It is his business to arrange for the kind of
> experiences which, while they do not repel the student, but rather
> engage his activities are, nevertheless, more than immediately enjoy-
> able since they promote having desirable future experiences. Just
> as no man lives or dies to himself, so no experience lives and dies
> to itself. Wholly independent of desire or intent, every experience
> lives on in further experiences. Hence the central problem of an
> education based upon experience is to select the kind of present
> experiences that live fruitfully and creatively in subsequent experi-
> ences. (LW.13.13)

Note the positive point, which is easy to miss in this passage. It is
important that an educational experience—to be a *quality* one—should
be immediately agreeable to the student. This is not to say—as has been
stressed before—that the experience should be easy or merely fun. But,
the experience should be an engaging one, and this should be immediately apparent to the teacher and a sensitive classroom observer.[20] The
students are interested, they are appropriately challenged, and they see
the point behind the work that they are doing. They take ownership of

their learning and are visibly thinking and actively creating.[21] According to Dewey, that this is happening is "obvious and easy to judge," but it doesn't mean it is easy to create classrooms where this happens, and it doesn't mean that positive engagement is the end of the story. Not only does this learning have to be tied to ambitious and meaningful learning goals, but it has to meet the far more difficult test of preparing students for future growth.

As Dewey reminds us, "no experience lives and dies to itself . . . every experience lives on in further experience," and so: "the central problem of an education based upon experience is to select the kind of present experiences that live fruitfully and creatively in subsequent experiences." This is the meaning of educative experience: "the kind of present experiences that live fruitfully and creatively in subsequent experiences." As we will see in the next section, when we create engaging and interesting present experiences for students, we are doing our best to prepare them for fruitful and creative subsequent experiences.

## Reconstructing the Dualism: The Educational Present as Engaging and Preparatory

The existence and relative popularity of the television show *Are You Smarter Than a Fifth Grader?* is one of those obvious commentaries on schooling: In school we spend a lot of time, energy, and stress learning information that is forgotten soon after a test is taken. And, while we can all laugh along as adults are beaten on simple quizzes of information that current fifth graders are learning, we can't miss the point that we subject children to a preparatory education that fails to prepare them—and maybe this is putting it too harshly—for little more than hoping to advance up and out of formal schooling. If we are compelling children to sit for high stakes testing on material that is important to know, then why is it that we aren't deeply concerned that, shortly after graduation, this information vanishes from the heads of children? We are surely making a lot of noise around the idea that America is "a nation at risk" when it comes to education, but we have to wonder if we are looking for reform in all the wrong places, especially if a silly television show makes it clear what we already know: School is often a game that one plays to advance with the least amount of work for the greatest possible reward.[22]

This is not a new point; Dewey (2008h) makes it in *Experience and Education*:

> Almost everyone has had occasion to look back upon his school days and wonder what has become of the knowledge he was supposed to have amassed during his years of schooling, and why it is that the technical skills he acquired have to be learned over again in changed form in order to stand him in good stead. Indeed, he is lucky who does not find that in order to make progress, in order to go ahead intellectually, he does not have to unlearn much of what he learned in school. These questions cannot be disposed of by saying that the subjects were not actually learned, for they were learned at least sufficiently to enable a pupil to pass examinations in them. One trouble is that the subject-matter in question was learned in isolation; it was put, as it were, in a water-tight compartment. When the question is asked, then, what has become of it, where has it gone to, the right answer is that it is still there in the special compartment in which it was originally stowed away. If exactly the same conditions recurred as those under which it was acquired, it would also recur and be available. But it was segregated when it was acquired and hence is so disconnected from the rest of experience that it is not available under the actual conditions of life. It is contrary to the laws of experience that learning of this kind, no matter how thoroughly engrained at the time, should give genuine preparation. (LW.13.28–29)

Here we see Dewey describing the importance of the process of *transfer* in learning.[23] We often forget what we learned during school because it stays compartmentalized. While Dewey is optimistic that we can reopen that compartment if we return to a school-like setting, he shows the ultimate futility of this type of learning because this learning "is not available under the actual conditions of life" and so does not "give genuine preparation." For schooling to prepare us for life, the information we learn in school must be available to us when we need it.

Here is the challenge for the new education Dewey advocates: Educators must find ways to help students *transfer* what they are learning in school to out of school contexts or to other subjects within school. This is why project-based learning, or learning that approximates authentic practice is so important. If a student is engaged in *real* work, not just work that supposedly prepares us to do this work one day, they are prepared for meaningful futures, because they are engaged in meaningful work now. An excellent example of this can be found in an Edutopia video that looks at performance-based assessment in Hampton High School in Allison Park, Pennsylvania.[24] At Hampton, students in a precalculus class play the role of air traffic controllers in a simulated disaster situation, and they must apply what they learned in the math classroom to meet the challenges and solve problems that resemble challenges and problems that one might face in the world. These students are clearly not all preparing to become air traffic controllers, but they are being prepared to use the math they are learning in the classroom outside of the classroom and in future situations. It is powerful learning experiences like this that allow students to *transfer* what they are learning outside of the classroom. Learning experiences like this are both engaging and preparatory, and they are what Dewey has in mind when he calls for an education that is responsive to the present.

In addition to making sure that what students are learning transfers, Dewey focuses on the affective dimension of learning.[25] In particular, Dewey reminds us of the importance of the attitudes that are formed in students while they are learning and the impact it has on their futures. If a student is generally engaged and interested in the work of learning, she is more likely to take up that work in the future. By contrast, if the student sees learning as drudgery, or if she feels inadequate to do the work of learning, it is likely that she will avoid that work in the future. Here is how Dewey (2008h) puts the point in *Experience and Education*:

> Nor does failure in preparation end at this point. Perhaps the greatest of all pedagogical fallacies is the notion that a person learns only the particular thing he is studying at the time. Collateral learning in the way of formation of enduring attitudes, of likes and dislikes, may be

and often is much more important than the spelling lesson or lesson in geography or history that is learned. For these attitudes are fundamentally what count in the future. The most important attitude that can be formed is that of desire to go on learning. If impetus in this direction is weakened instead of being intensified, something much more than mere lack of preparation takes place. The pupil is actually robbed of native capacities which otherwise would enable him to cope with the circumstances that he meets in the course of his life. We often see persons who have had little schooling and in whose case the absence of set schooling proves to be a positive asset. They have at least retained their native common sense and power of judgment, and its exercise in the actual conditions of living has given them the precious gift of ability to learn from the experiences they have. What avail is it to win prescribed amounts of information about geography and history, to win ability to read and write, if in the process the individual loses his own soul: loses his appreciation of things worth while, of the values to which these things are relative; if he loses desire to apply what he has learned and, above all, loses the ability to extract meaning from his future experiences as they occur? (LW.13.29)

This is one of many moments in Dewey's prose where his even tone belies a deep passion. When reading a work like *Experience and Education* it is easy to feel that one must just try to keep up with the thinking and argumentation. But, when we read this way, we can miss just how impassioned about education Dewey is.[26]

Here Dewey is telling us in no uncertain terms that school robs children and causes them to lose their souls. When we don't focus on the present in education, we may feel like we are gaining a future world, but the reality is we are losing the soul of the learner; a soul that may be hardened to learning for a very long time because of what transpires in our schools and our classrooms. This passage is rich, and I want to focus on three main ideas Dewey is expressing here.

The first is the significance of collateral learning. Though a teacher may be able to gain the compliance of students and even get "results" because of this compliance, we have to wonder about the long-term impact of this type of teaching. A brief foray into sports may help. I imagine we might know athletes who were very successful on the field, but once their careers were over, they were so turned off to athletics that they were unable to engage in healthy physical activities. They had coaches who pushed them to get results, but who didn't take the long view, who didn't consider the collateral dimension of learning. By contrast, we may know athletes who weren't entirely successful in college or high school athletics and who had coaches who didn't produce exceptional teams, but these athletes look back fondly at their practices and so continue to engage in physical activities because the collateral aspect of their learning was extremely positive.

As Dewey writes, the "most important attitude that can be formed is that of desire to go on learning." It is absolutely important that we keep this in mind as teachers. The research paper our student is writing for us in ninth grade is not the last paper that the child is ever going to write. Though the citations in the paper might not be perfect or the research exhaustive enough, these cannot be our only focus. As we continue to improve the student's developing skills as a researcher, we can wonder: Is the process of researching making the child excited to write the next paper? In our feedback on drafts and final papers, we should balance our desire for the student to write the best possible paper with a desire that the child grow in her own interest as a researcher.

I appreciate how teacher and author Cris Tovani (2011) is an advocate for, and a practitioner of, feedback that fortifies. Her feedback is meant to improve how her students write, but it also fortifies them and excites them to do the difficult and interesting work of continuous improvement as a writer. When we focus on the quality of a student's present learning experience, we are able to see very clearly that how a child feels during learning is not a minor matter. In our desire to get the best from students, we cannot forget that our best ally in learning is the student herself. As educators, I hope we have all experienced the joy that comes when our students are self-directed and in control of their own learning. Students seek our feedback because they are excited and want to improve; they do the work out of self-motivation and not out of a begrudging and mis-educative sense of duty to the game of school. Though some who have not experienced this may find the vision hopelessly naïve, for those who have had moments like this in the classroom, it encourages us to want all of the work that happens in our classrooms to be like this.

The second point that Dewey makes in the long passage quoted above is that schooling can rob students of their native capacities, and that for these students no schooling would often be better than the schooling they receive given the damage caused. In fact: "We often see persons who have had little schooling and in whose case the absence of set schooling proves to be a positive asset." This is a remarkable quote from someone who is a major advocate of public education, and puts Dewey in close company with advocates of unschooling, a position that is worth appreciating as a means to reforming schooling. Father and unschooling advocate Ben Hewitt (2014) makes the case that schooling often kills creativity and self-motivation. More, its promise of being necessary preparation for a successful future is often a hollow one. Because his children are not subjected to formal schooling, they are forced to take responsibility for their own learning and thereby grow in self-trust and self-motivation. As an unschooling parent Hewitt finds that the freedom from school his children experience fits Dewey's insight that

> we often see persons who have had little schooling and in whose case the absence of set schooling proves to be a positive asset. They have at least retained their native common sense and power of judgment, and its exercise in the actual conditions of living has given them the precious gift of ability to learn from the experiences they have.

This is a telling indictment of formal schooling. Nonetheless, Dewey would be adamantly against unschooling. Not only do most parents not have the resources to unschool, but unschooling is often mis-educative and it almost always limits the contacts of life that children have. For a democracy to flourish, children must leave their homes and come together into the social life of school. It is through public education that we learn from others with different backgrounds and beliefs, and through this learning forge a new identity and a new sociality.[27] But, school has the obligation to make it so that a child's native common sense and power of judgment are not deadened and destroyed by school, but opened to learning from new children and new opportunities only made possible by public education. For Dewey, school is not a preparation for future citizenship, but school itself is its own society, and children learn to become citizens of this environment quite quickly. If the school environment allows for bullying to occur unchallenged, students learn that this is what life is like. A school where students aren't challenged or supported teaches students that this is what life is like. By contrast, school can do what unschooling does at its best: It can promote self-trust and self-motivation to learn. More, it can bring students from different backgrounds together and teach that mutual accommodation and growth can happen when an environment of trust and respect is built and cultivated. This is what it would mean to not defer meaningful life and work to the future, to live educationally in the present.

In absence of an educational present, we get to Dewey's third point: "What avail is it to win prescribed amounts of information about geography and history, to win ability to read and write, if in the process the individual loses his own soul." We must be honest about what formal education produces, and see that it not only can rob students of their native capacities, but it can indeed cause a student to lose the soul of learning. Here we can see the quote going in a few directions. We may all know students who play the game of school so well that they lose out on learning. These students may take and pass five, six, ten Advanced Placement tests in high school, but are burned out after graduation and so fail to take any advantage of what college can offer. Or those students who are so grade-obsessed that they never experience the *pleasure* of learning.[28] We can also think of students who feel less-than because of their schooling experience. Because they fail to perform up to an external standard and never learn to develop an internal one, they feel inadequate and so miss out on the world of learning that would be open to them had they not been put through the emotional wringer of their schooling experience.

I don't think we can ever appreciate this point enough. Schooling should ensure that every student who experiences school is more interested in learning because of her schooling experience. Any schooling experience that fails this test should be judged something of a failure. It doesn't matter if a student gains a great deal of information and admittance to an elite school. If she isn't interested in her continued growth and if her schooling doesn't prepare her to take an interest in what the contacts of life have to offer, then she hasn't received an education worthy of the name. An education worthy of the name leaves us interested in learning more, passionately growing in and through the soul of learning.

The soul of learning may seem overwrought as a term, but it best captures what Dewey means by living fully in the present moment. Tolstoy, and following him Wittgenstein, makes the strong case that eternal life belongs to whomever lives fully in the present, and that we are good only as we are living—now, in this moment—in goodness. Goodness cannot wait; it can—and must—be experienced now. This is strong language, but listen to Dewey (2008h) as he continues his thinking in *Experience and Education*:

> What, then, is the true meaning of preparation in the educational scheme? In the first place, it means that a person, young or old, gets out of his present experience all that there is in it for him at the time in which he has it. When preparation is made the controlling end, then the potentialities of the present are sacrificed to a suppositious future. When this happens, the actual preparation for the future is missed or distorted. The ideal of using the present simply to get ready for the future contradicts itself. It omits, and even shuts out, the very conditions by which a person can be prepared for his future. We always live at the time we live and not at some other time, and only by extracting at each present time the full meaning of each

present experience are we prepared for doing the same thing in the future. This is the only preparation which in the long run amounts to anything. (LW.13.29–30)

This, again, is an impassioned and beautiful paean to what education can and should be. We sacrifice so much to a supposititious future instead of living fully in the present. Instead of enjoying and becoming enriched by what is happening now, we look to the future. As Dewey puts it, we should be "extracting at each present time the full meaning of each present experience," this is a good in itself—to be sure—but it is also the only way to ensure that "we are prepared for doing the same thing in the future." Why would we think a mediocre experience in the present will prepare us for excellence in the future? Why don't we attempt to live excellence now; doesn't that seem like the most likely path to living excellently in the future?

Putting it this directly may make this point an obvious one, but when we turn our attention back to our own schooling and the way that we relate to time and our present, I think we might be able to see the gulf that separates Dewey's ideal from our reality. How many times have we told ourselves things like: Once I graduate college I will be able to do the work I really want to do, or after I get my advanced degree I will start doing the work that really matters, or after I get tenure I will finally be free to do the work that I've always envisioned myself doing. As we continue deferring the work we would like to do, we are learning and deepening habits that will only make it harder to do that type of work in the future.

The same might be said of parenting. We can keep telling ourselves we will be a certain type of parent once a certain landmark is met (once a child can talk, or once a child is in school, or once a child reaches a certain grade), but we can keep deferring until we find that our own child is a parent herself and the present we hoped for remains as far away now as it was when the child was first born. Wanting something to happen in the future, wanting to live meaningfully in the future is not preparing for the future. Only by extracting the full meaning of our present will we be prepared to do the same in the future.[29] As educators, it is our duty to make the present as full and fully meaningful as possible. Though we may feel that the call to prepare students is overwhelming and that it would be irresponsible not to follow the well-worn path of mere preparation, Dewey's thinking is meant to fortify us to become advocates of the present and not deferrers and devotees to a future good that will never arrive because, as Dewey teaches, the future good and the meaningful future are only created by those who are attempting to live meaningfully and well now, in the present.

## Cultivating the Pedagogical Imagination

Instead of labeling this section "implications" and talking from a height down to practice, the work I want to do is the mutual thinking that I often call "cultivating the pedagogical imagination." I use the term pedagogical imagination to get at the fact that teaching is something that one can learn to get better at, but so much of working together to become a better teacher depends on the *person* of the teacher and how she sees the world. I have known preservice teachers who see the classroom and its possibilities as fixed—this is what can be done, this is what children can do—and I have had the good fortune to work with teachers who've been in the classroom over thirty years and see all the possibility that can be cultivated, and all the room there is for growth. This quality is what I've come to think of as the pedagogical imagination: It is the way that two teachers can look at the same classroom, in the same school, with the same children and see two radically different worlds.[30]

What I hope for myself, for my future teachers and the teachers I work with, is that we can see how important it is to work on the pedagogical imagination. Cultivating the pedagogical imagination is not to demand ready-made solutions to our problems that come from experts or fellow practitioners; it is, instead, to think with others; drawing on our own experience, testing and learning from the experience and thoughts of others and coming to create, almost poetically (Hansen, 2004), a new way of seeing and working in our classrooms. Though I agree with recent developments in teacher education that it is important to develop "core practices" or "practice-based" approaches to teaching and teacher education (Forzani, 2014; Kennedy, 2016), because many of our students graduate from a teacher education program and struggle to *enact* what they learned in teacher education (Kennedy, 1999; Grossman, McDonald, Hammermas, & Ronfeldt, 2008) it is also the case that there is an *imagination* gap in our graduates (and in teaching more generally), and this is also important.

Works like David Hansen's (2001) that ask us to explore the moral dimensions of the teaching practice and that ask us to consider how our ideals deeply impact how we teach and interact with students, I believe, are important complements and must be a part of any practice-based approach to teaching. As Dewey (2008h) writes, "Every genuine experience has an active side which changes in some degree the objective conditions under which experiences are had" (LW.13.22). This is significant, but underappreciated, when we think about teaching and learning to teach. Every genuine experience—we teach well or poorly; we respond humanely or fail to respond humanly; we have a true respect for and interest in our students or fear, distrust, and are closed off to them—changes the *objective* conditions under which experiences are had. I think it is easy to imagine two teachers who are doing roughly the same thing—following the same teaching move they learned during their teacher education—and yet the impact of those moves having very different results.[31] The way the teacher ensouls or inspirits her work is not a minor thing. Students can tell when a teacher believes in him or her and can feel the passion that the teacher has almost before the teacher says a single word.[32] The human dimension of teaching makes it so that it is very difficult to study teaching because of the irreducibility and nonequivalence of teachers. Each teacher is unique and any suggestions for improving the practice of teaching should take this idea very seriously (Hansen, 2018).

For this reason, I will avoid offering moves that can be generally or universally applied in teaching, and opt instead for us to think about our own irreducibility as human educators, and consider how we might inspirit Dewey's thinking in ways that work given our nonequivalence with other teachers. There will certainly be much we hold in common and ideas that we can share, but it is also important to consider what Dewey's thinking means for who we are, who we teach, what we value. With this as an introduction, I want to highlight some key themes from this chapter as it relates to teaching.

I think one of the most important questions we can ask ourselves as educators is: What habits are our students learning in our classrooms? Importantly, we should consider the direct academic habits being taught, as well as the "collateral" habits being instilled. I think this can be a difficult question for an educator to ask, because it takes a great scope of vision to respond to it effectively. That is, each day in class can be an experiment with wonder, with discovery, with democracy, with hope. A teacher who is alive to these possibilities creates a very different learning environment for students than a teacher who doesn't see the classroom through these lenses.

For almost every activity a teacher does in class, she can ask the simple question: What are the short- and long-term impacts of this activity? Will students be more likely to take an interest in learning because of this activity? Will students feel empowered to take control of their learning because of this activity? What does this activity teach students about who they are as learners, who their peers are as learners, and who their teacher is and what she cares about? At the very least, I think that these questions should be constant companions in the classroom, if we want to take Dewey's thinking seriously. Again, we can take any activity we have students do—watching a movie because we just finished standardized testing or are waiting for a break; putting students into groups so that the "more advanced" students can teach, coach and control the "more difficult students"; using presentations created by textbook companies and then giving students the tests created by these companies—and ask ourselves the simple question: How will this experience live on in the future experience of my students? Is this experience going to make more meaningful learning in the future more—or less—likely?

I don't mean to add pressure to teaching by asking these types of questions.[33] Instead, I hope they inspire an activation of, or deepened connection to, the pedagogical imagination. Dewey reminds us that teachers are often told that a given activity is *necessary* as preparation, but as I hope to have shown, Dewey is correct to assert that many of these so-called necessary activities fail to accomplish the goal of preparation, and often set in place habits that are mis-educative. For this reason, I find Dewey inspiring because the questions he causes us to ask allow us to see that our practices are not *fixed* in place, and empower us to find alternatives to practices that are not as educative as they could be; practices that don't inspire students and don't inspire us to do the teaching that we would really like to do.

Wondering about the value of showing students a certain video, or rethinking using a certain worksheet, or questioning whether test-preparation only consists in taking practice tests may not lead to a radical reconstruction of our educational practices tomorrow, but it does affect the pedagogical imagination now, and it does cause us to see possibilities for change where we may have seen fixities. This is the thinking that Dewey hopes we begin now, and this thinking leads us to grow and develop as learners and teachers.

Relatedly, Dewey wants to inspire creativity by having us teachers think about the following question: What will a student's future experience with this topic look like? This is a related question, because it allows us to see the academic and collateral dimensions of learning. Take any topic we are teaching or plan to teach and think about how a student will feel about this topic in the future and how prepared she will be to engage meaningfully with that topic. One of my greatest joys as a college professor is when a student emails me a semester or a year after a course and tells me that she heard something on the news or read something in the paper on education reform and could see through the superficial analysis offered by the report and that the news report was just the reminder she needed to re-engage with the topic.

It's a small example, but I felt the same way as a high school English teacher. When I first introduced my ninth graders to American poetry, for example, I wanted to teach just enough to get the students interested and able to do some independent work with poetry, but not too much that reading poetry became a puzzle to be dropped once the right interpretation was divined.[34] Like Bruner's (1960) spiral, I saw engaging with something as important as poetry as something that a student should keep coming back to, and each time coming with more understanding given an accrual of learning and life experience. Making poetry too complex and difficult at the outset could turn a student off to poetry, but not trusting a student to have a genuine experience with poetry often did the same. Teachers need to create an environment where students can have an appropriately challenging and engaging experience with poetry, an experience that leads students to feel that poetry is not confined within the game of school, but something that can be a part of their own life. I hope we can envision examples from our own teaching. Take a moment and think about how you hope your students engage with a few of the things you most value in your curriculum five years from now. Is your teaching helping you bring about that vision? If not, what can be done? What can we do to make it more likely that our students continue engaging with what is most valuable in our curriculum years after they leave our classrooms and the confines of formal education?

In addition to asking these questions, questions that are very closely tied to daily life in our classrooms, we can ask the relatively bigger question as to what it would mean to extract the fullest possible meaning from each present moment. To start, can we facilitate this experience for students, if we haven't given a good deal of thought to how we extract or fail to extract everything that the present moment offers us. To put it another way, how often do we feel in the state that many, following the work of Csikszentmihalyi (1990), label as "flow"? That is, how often do we feel so deeply engaged in what we are doing that we both feel lost in the work and absolutely attuned to it? How do we get into, and stay, in that state? Following Dewey, how is it that we become so interested in all the contacts that life offers at every single moment that we are never bored; that we are always finding new avenues of interest and paths toward continuous growth?

These questions aren't meant as judgments, but provocations to make more of the present (something we all can always do). More, they are questions that are meant to help us see our students in a new light.

How can our classrooms be spaces where students feel that their present experiences are not being squandered, but being made the most of? A place of learning, where students—even though they are compelled to be there—would *choose* to be in the classroom given the quality of the experience, educative and engaging, they are having.

There is a great deal of interest in helping the general public (Dixit, 2008) and teachers more specifically (Jennings, 2015) become more mindful and more able to live fully in the present. This is a salutary development, and school can be a space where we can find freedom from a world of mere preparation, and reclaim the joy of learning and the joy of being in the company of youth. I am not saying that teachers at all levels are not under a tremendous amount of pressure, but I am hopeful that—to borrow a beautiful phrase from "God's Grandeur" by Gerard Manley Hopkins (1877)—"There lives the dearest freshness deep down things." That is, despite everything, the human educative relationship holds nascent within it so much potential, always, and we can access that potential by being appreciative of it in each present moment where we have the gift of working with young people.

We need to keep coming back around to those things that really matter, drown out the din that we *must* prepare students in a certain way, and remember that the best preparation for a quality future is making the attempt to live well now. Instead of rushing to that next activity, appreciate the engaged students in front of us now. Instead of worrying about covering more material, appreciate what it means to sit with something and uncover its depths.[35] Instead of hoping to do good teaching once certain barriers are removed, start thinking about the aspects of that teaching you can do now.

For Dewey, this is the important point: Wishing something is not enough. Too often we defer in the name of some future good, but in education as we defer we lose the present. Our students can't wait until we figure things out or until we live under whatever ideal of educational policy we are hoping for. Students deserve our present attention; the quality of attention we bring to our students, in the present, matters: It shows them that they matter to us.[36] As well, we must endeavor to make any activity we do in our classrooms as engaging *and* educative as possible. While we will fall short of this ideal, we cannot give up on the ideal, and we must do everything in our power to endeavor to enact this ideal as often as possible. Though our present may fall short of the ideal, we should be heartened by the fact because it means that we must participate in the type of moral and intellectual growth we hope for our students. Sharing in this process of growth is good for us and our teaching. In the next chapter I focus on the importance of cultivating the ideal of living in the present while also showing the importance of continuous experimentation on our way to enacting that ideal.

**CHAPTER 3**

# Ideals and Experiments: Creating the Present

Hoping is not enough. Although John Dewey is often dismissed as overly idealistic, this criticism—aspiring to be a tough-minded and realistic one[1]—is often just the opposite, and almost always fails to appreciate the role that *work* plays in Dewey's pragmatism. That is, it is easy to dismiss Dewey's analysis of education on sociological or descriptive grounds, because we know that schools and students are not the way that Dewey describes them in his work. But, Dewey's project, while grounded in reality, is largely a *normative* and not a *descriptive* one; that is, Dewey writes about how schools *should* be, and then urges us to collaboratively and democratically create conditions that will bring better forms of education into being. His work is meant to encourage us to live the possibilities we see unrealized in our classrooms.

As I briefly discuss in chapter two, it is important for readers of Dewey to appreciate his insight in *Experience and Education* when he writes, "Every genuine experience has an active side which changes in some degree the objective conditions under which experiences are had" (LW.13.22). As we begin working to realize our ideals in education, the very objective conditions of education will change. As these conditions change, we will need to examine what the changing conditions mean for our ideals and for the ways in which we experiment to realize those ideals. The process is anything but idealistic in the pejorative sense; it is an empirically driven and creative process. If we want students to extract the fullest meaning from their educational presents, we have to: (1) see how far we are from our ideals; (2) experiment to create the conditions where students can live more meaningfully in the present; (3) study the impact of our experiments; and (4) see where we stand in relation to our ideals and see how—if at all—the objective conditions in which we are working change.[2]

It might help to make this process more concrete with a negative and a positive example. To take the negative example first, a popular educational ideal became to leave no child behind when it came to education. Though the goal itself may have had—and still may have—the broadest possible support, it takes work and experiments to realize the ideal. There are many directions one might go in leaving no child behind, but as we know from recent history, the United States decided to use high-stakes standardized assessment to realize the ideal. So, using the steps outlined above, policies like No Child Left Behind (1) used standardized assessment to show where students stood academically. These tests revealed that there were students who—given the results of these tests—were falling behind their peers and achievement benchmarks. Using the results of these tests, teachers and schools moved to step (2).

Here we see wide variations. Some classrooms (a) used ambitious instruction to help students learn material, hoping that this would in turn lead to higher scores; other schools (b) did more direct test-preparation, hoping that this would lead to higher scores. This then leads to step (3): In schools that chose option (a), teachers and leaders could see if their students learned the material in a way that allowed them to be successful on the tests or they could decide: (i) that the tests were invalid measures of what students actually know and understand or (ii) their students didn't learn the material or (iii) the students know the material but need additional test preparation. In option (b), teachers and leaders could see if test-preparation led to higher test scores and then decide where to go from there. In either case, the objective conditions of education changed. In scenario (a), teachers experimented with pedagogy and were able to see the impacts of this pedagogy on standardized assessment. In scenario (b), school became test preparation. This leads to step (4). We are only now coming to terms with the full impact of using standardized assessments as the means by which we realize the ideal of making sure that American public education leaves no child behind. I think it is safe to say, at the least, that the objective conditions of schooling change when children see schooling as tantamount to test preparation; when the results of standardized assessments are used to make determinations of teaching quality and school effectiveness; when terms like test anxiety become a much larger part of the lexicon.

As Diane Ravitch (2010) has passionately argued, though the ideal of leaving no child behind may have been a good one, the experiments we used to realize that ideal have led us farther away from the ideal and have often created new problems that did not exist before we attempted to improve education for all students. Our recent attempts to realize our ideals through standardized testing lead us to a place where, hopefully, we will learn from this experiment without giving up on the ideal of making public schools places where all students make progress toward ambitious learning goals.[3] We can still hold to the ideal, but we should use different experiments to realize it.

The point of bringing up this example is not for the sake of discussing standardized assessment, but to show one case—a negative one as I present it—of working to realize educational ideals. Another example—albeit smaller, different, and positive—is to think about a teacher who believes in differentiated instruction and who experiments with it in her classroom. This teacher is convinced that there are a range of learners in her classroom (they have different readiness levels for each topic she teaches; they have different interests), and she would like to make her pedagogy *responsive* to this. Her ideal is to make her pedagogy responsive to student differences. So, she experiments with differentiated instruction. When teaching what she thinks will be new to many students, she does a preassessment to see what students already know about the material. When she finds a range of readiness with respect to the particular topic she plans to teach, she groups students by that readiness. Students already familiar with the topic are given one learning experience; students with no familiarity are given another; students with misconceptions are given another altogether.

The work that students are given is not easier or harder; it is the most appropriately challenging work the teacher can come up with given what she knows about where the students are and the goal she has in mind for the class. After this assignment—or, more likely, a series of assignments like this—she can gauge the effectiveness of her instruction. She learns how the students respond to differentiated instruction, and learns when she succeeds and fails to effectively help each student realize her learning goal. Regardless, the objective conditions of her classroom have changed. Her students are now in a differentiated learning environment, and there will be obvious and not-so-obvious implications of this fact. It is her responsibility, as an experimenter, to be mindful of the range of implications set in motion because of her changing pedagogy and to make decisions based on what she finds. She may find that students respond better to readiness differentiation on certain topics or types of assignments, and she may find that she falls into the habit of making assignments easier for students instead of making them *appropriately* challenging. She may also find, after years of experimenting, that the ideal of differentiated instruction is indeed too idealistic or not as effective as other forms of instruction. Or, what I have found to be more common in my experience as a teacher educator, she may find that the ideal of differentiated instruction remains an inspiring one; an ideal that allows her to continuously experiment, grow, and learn as an educator.[4]

She will never become the perfect differentiator; her classroom will never be an ideal differentiated learning space for every student, but the ideal allows her to see possibilities in her classroom that inspire her to move closer to the ideal in ways that are educative for her students and for herself. Working toward an ideal doesn't mean being tied to perfectionism—it only means that one is inspired to keep learning and growing as an educator.

Again, the point here is not to debate the merits of differentiated instruction, but to think about what learning looks like when we are attempting to experimentally enact an educational ideal. The process isn't an easy or neat one, and this is why the term "implementation" can feel jarring or off-putting to anyone who works in classrooms. We don't implement an educational solution; we work to realize goals with very real children given very real constraints and possibilities. More important, as we try new things, the objective conditions in the classroom change. Children form new expectations; children form new desires and resistances given what we are trying to do; and we learn new things about our students, our teaching, and our classrooms as we work to change the learning environment. We see possibilities and limitations that weren't apparent before we began our experiments.

All of this brings us back to Dewey's ideal of extracting the fullest possible meaning from the educational present. It is important to realize that living more fully in the present is an ideal, and as an ideal it is something that we must experiment our way toward. More, ideals get enacted in particular contexts, by particular teachers and with particular students. Fidelity in educational experiments, that is, measuring how true to an ideal a given implementation of an educational intervention is, must by necessity be problematic (Missett & Foster, 2015). Even something as seemingly simplistic as assessing the impact of using something like a single iPad application will be difficult to measure across educational contexts, because the students using the application and the teachers implementing the new technology will have different feelings, experiences, hopes, and fears with technology in general and using classroom technology in particular. This is not to say that we cannot learn from each other and our differences. How other teachers use differentiation, even if they use it differently than I do and even though they have different students than I do, will help me understand and grow in my own teaching, for example. My intention is to caution us against giving up on something because of the experiences of others and to caution us against believing that someone has found a magical formula that we can simply implement in our unique contexts and expect to get the same results.

Living more fully in the present is not something we've tried enough to give up on, or something that we've achieved and so can simply implement in our classrooms. We are still at the stage where we must hold it as an ideal and work—diligently, creatively, and with a great deal of openness to learning from experience—to realize that ideal through experimentation.

I will discuss in more detail below how Dewey's thinking on ideals is in fact quite close to what we now call nonideal theory (Mills, 2005; Anderson, 2010), but for the moment I turn to the summary of Dewey's discussion of aims in chapter eight of *Democracy and Education* as a way of further appreciating what it means to work toward an educational ideal. Dewey (2008e) writes:

> A true aim is thus opposed at every point to an aim which is imposed upon a process of action from without. The latter is fixed and rigid; it is not a stimulus to intelligence in the given situation, but is an externally dictated order to do such and such things. Instead of connecting directly with present activities, it is remote, divorced from the means by which it is to be reached. Instead of suggesting a freer and better balanced activity, it is a limit set to activity. In education, the currency of these externally imposed aims is responsible for the emphasis put upon the notion of preparation for a remote future and for rendering the work of both teacher and pupil mechanical and slavish. (MW.9.117)

I imagine this line of thinking might resonate with teachers. How often is our work dictated from the outside: Aims are given to us, and we are expected to "implement" them. When we don't select our own aims, when we aren't passionately behind their realization, when they don't account for our context and our students, then they don't lead to transformation; instead, they lead to mere conformity, making our work and the work of our students "mechanical and slavish."

A way out of this situation is to consciously select our own educational aims. We must give ourselves our own goals, and then our work moves beyond mere compliance to a striving to realize the world we would like to live.[5] More, when we reflectively select our own aims, our work becomes flexible. Think back to the time when we were first learning something that doesn't come naturally to us—skiing, skating, cooking, knitting—and, at the beginning, we don't feel comfortable doing the work. We follow the rules or moves we were taught mechanically; it isn't until we gain some facility with what we are learning that we can make it our own and so become creative and flexible as to how we respond to problem situations and opportunities. When we don't have a certain ingredient, we can improvise; we hit a patch of ice while skiing, we adjust. This is what self-selected aims and ideals allow us to do in the classroom. We set a goal of helping our students be more active learners, and—to facilitate this end—we plan a lesson that uses an interactive web-based technology. But—how often does this happen—our students can't connect to the wireless, or the computer cart isn't where it should be. If we aren't fully in control of our educational aims, then the loss of the technology—the means of realizing our aims—keeps us from our aims. By contrast, if we remember that the aim is active learning—the technology remains a mere means of achieving it—then we can be flexible and still realize this aim, even if it calls for some quick thinking and creativity on our part.

Our aims are realized in the messiness and beauty of the present moment. Technology breaks, students have bad days, we have bad days, and things happen in our communities that impact life in our classrooms. At the same time, students say the most insightful and wonderful things, students show deep care for each other when we least expect it, things happen in the news or our communities that have an immediate and meaningful connection to our classrooms. When we are in control of our educational aims, we can live more fully in the present, because we know where we want students to head and so we can use every moment as a chance to get them there.

This is why I find it both important and fascinating that Dewey closes his thinking on educational aims by reminding us of the importance of the educational present. He writes, "In education, the currency of these externally imposed aims is responsible for the emphasis put upon the notion of preparation for a remote future and for rendering the work of both teacher and pupil mechanical and slavish." We lose the educational present, in large part, because we don't do enough to stand for the present. Instead of developing our own aims and advocating for them, we can fall into the pattern of accepting aims imposed from outside, most notably the idea that the aim of education is to merely prepare students for the future. But, as we've seen in the previous chapter, this approach to preparation does not prepare, and worse, it has collateral—often damaging—impacts on students in the present and the future.

This is why Dewey spends all of chapter 8 in *Democracy and Education* discussing educational aims and their importance. When we don't set aims, they are set for us. That is, when we don't diligently consider what it actually means to prepare students for the future—in and outside of school—we can default to the given view that what is done in schools is adequate preparation. But, when we begin considering the lasting impact of what passes for preparation in our schools, then we begin to see that something needs to change. Change is hard—as Dewey discusses at length in chapter 4 of *Democracy and Education*—because what were once flexible habits that helped us achieve meaningful aims can harden into habituated tracks of thinking and teaching that don't do the work we claim or hope to do. Our classrooms begins working in certain ways, almost despite our intentions. We've probably all heard of a veteran teacher who gives the advice that you figure things out the first few years and then run on autopilot from there. But, when we do that, we are not actively working to realize meaningful educational aims; instead we are succumbing to habits that don't allow us to take fullest advantage of the possibilities presented by the present. This is why Dewey wants us to move out of a default position if we are in one or avoid defaulting if we can. Instead, we must set aims and assess whether our thinking and our work are moving us closer to—or farther away from—those aims.

This will be the focus of the next sections. We will look at key passages from *Democracy and Education* and *Experience and Education* to more fully appreciate the importance of being intentional about our educational aims. As we've started to see in this section, we can only extract the fullest possibilities from the present if we are looking to do this. Gilliam, Maupin, Reyes, Accavitti, and Shic (2016) make something like this point when they discuss implicit bias and preschool teachers. The researchers designed a study where they asked a group of preschool teachers to look for misbehavior on a video of a preschool classroom (there was no misbehavior in the video). While the video was playing, the researchers tracked where the teachers looked. What they found was that the teachers were far more likely to look at black male students than any other group of students. They used this finding to hypothesize that more black males are suspended and expelled from school—starting as early as kindergarten—because that is where the teachers are looking for misbehavior, not because black males are more prone to misbehave than other students.

I bring up this study because I want to assert something like the opposite side of a study like this, with reference to Dewey's thinking on the educational present. When our aim is to extract the fullest meaning from the present, our classrooms are charged with significance and possibility; just as when we are looking for misbehavior our classrooms are charged with a spirit of surveillance and distrust. To echo a paraphrase of Wittgenstein (1921/1999), the world of the hopeful classroom teacher is a different world altogether than the classroom of the nonbelieving teacher. When a teacher wants the present moment to be engaging and educative for each of her students, she quite literally sees things that a teacher who doesn't believe that all her students can learn will never see and claim can never exist. An important prerequisite for doing the type of teaching that Dewey calls us to do is something like a change of heart, or conversation, or leap of faith that allows us to work to bring about worlds in our classrooms that we have yet to see and that some will claim do not and can never exist.[6] When we take this step, we set ambitious aims for our students and feel called and energized to activate as many resources as possible to realize that aim.

Though the idea of mandating that teachers have certain dispositions before they can teach is controversial and difficult to effectively assess and cultivate (Murrell, Diez, Feiman-Nemser, & Schussler, 2010), I am of the mind that—at heart—it is hard to call teaching anything like a (moral) profession if teachers in classrooms don't believe that every single student can learn and is deserving of the fullest possible educative experience that can be provided. As I will show in more detail in the following sections, we have a lot to gain as teachers by reclaiming the moral dimensions of our work, especially because reconnecting with the moral dimensions of teaching allows us to be the responsive educators every one of our students deserve.[7]

## Nothing is Deferred: On Moral and Mental Vacuums

Even if we do not hold explicit educational ideals, educational ideals will nonetheless always animate the life of our classrooms. Jackson, Boostrom, and Hansen (1998) offer an extraordinarily rich description and discussion of how almost everything that a teacher does in a classroom has a moral tone and a moral dimension. As I think about that book and teaching more generally, I am often reminded of a line from Emerson's (1841/1983a) "Self-Reliance," where he writes, "We pass for what we are. Character teaches above our wills. Men imagine that they communicate their virtue or vice only by overt actions, and do not see that virtue or vice emit a breath every moment" (p. 266). Even if we don't have explicit educational aims or ideals, our students know and feel them. And, if we only claim ideals—like equality—and don't live them, our students know that as well. From the way we respond to a student who is experiencing a hardship to the way we handle bullying to the way we grade and give feedback: Everything expresses what we value.[8]

It is deeply important that we think more about our values and work hard to bring our practices in line with those values.[9] Importantly, one can hold values in education nondogmatically and without succumbing to moralism.[10] Oftentimes the most moral people we know are those who aren't advertising their morality or shaming others in its name: They live their ideals and make them felt. It is important to remember and recall those teachers who made us most at home, engaged, and interested in learning, so that we can call to mind the type of moral lives we want to promote in classrooms. Again, it may be nothing explicit that these teachers do and say—it can simply be in the ways they make eye contact, or come prepared to do their work, or respond with flexibility and humor to problems—but their moral presence is present and felt nonetheless.

When we think about what we want to see in the educational presents of our students, we are forming our ideals and values, and this work is incredibly important because without it we leave our values to chance and inertia or have them imposed on us. If we want to extract the fullest and richest possibilities from the educational present, then we must make this our aim. Here is how Dewey (2008e) puts the point in *Democracy and Education*:

> School conditions favorable to this division of mind between avowed, public, and socially responsible undertakings, and private, ill-regulated, and suppressed indulgences of thought are not hard to find. What is sometimes called "stern discipline," i.e., external coercive pressure, has this tendency. Motivation through rewards extraneous to the thing to be done has a like effect. Everything that makes schooling merely preparatory (see p. 59) works in this direction. Ends being beyond the pupil's present grasp, other agencies have to be found to procure immediate attention to assigned tasks. Some responses are secured, but desires and affections not enlisted must find other outlets. Not less serious is exaggerated emphasis upon drill exercises designed to produce skill in action, independent of any engagement of thought—exercises having no purpose but the production of automatic skill. Nature abhors a mental vacuum. What do teachers imagine is happening to thought and emotion when the latter get no outlet in the things of immediate activity? Were they merely kept in temporary abeyance, or even only calloused, it would not be a matter of so much moment. But they are not abolished; they are not suspended; they are not suppressed—save with reference to the task in question. They follow their own chaotic and undisciplined course. What is native, spontaneous, and vital in mental reaction goes unused and untested, and the habits formed are such that these qualities become less and less available for public and avowed ends. (MW.9.185)

What I find fascinating about this passage is how it weaves together so many of the themes we've discussed up to this point and will continue to consider together. It is important to see that "everything that makes schooling merely preparatory" almost always has pernicious short- and long-term effects. Though "stern discipline" may give the appearance of being effective, in the short-term all that is gained is compliance, and—in the long-term—we graduate students who have an ill-formed sense that the most powerful authority is the one who demands and coerces the greatest compliance from the greatest number of people.

As we saw in the introduction, this sense can very easily lead us away from a belief in democracy and a movement toward authoritarianism. This line of thinking gets to what I see as a key to this passage, which is found in the middle, where Dewey writes, "Some responses are secured, but desires and affections not enlisted must find other outlets." Spoken like a very insightful teacher. When we demand compliance—of our children, of our students—do we really believe that we have eradicated or rooted out the desires that we would like to see altered or directed toward better ends? I believe Dewey is correct to worry that the desires are not erased; they just find other outlets. Students become sneakier; students learn new habits of disobedience; students spend so much time finding ways to get what they wanted to do originally that they are completely lost to whatever it is that we are trying to get them to do *after* we forced their compliance.

Dewey goes on to write: "Nature abhors a mental vacuum. What do teachers imagine is happening to thought and emotion when the latter get no outlet in the things of immediate activity?" This strikes me as a key insight. What do we think happens to all the energy that we are constraining by telling our students to wait—to defer, to put off—until some distant future that isn't lively enough to captivate the imagination and offer a channel for the energy that is waiting to burst through now, in this very moment?[11] Anyone who has taught knows the challenges and frustrations that come when students don't have an outlet for their immediate activity, just as teachers know the joy of channeling a child's creativity and curiosity into a project or task that is immediately engaging and which puts in place habits of mind that lead to deeper learning in the future.[12]

Just as nature abhors a mental vacuum, teachers should as well. When we aren't intentional about how we are directing the present energies of students, when we aren't moving that energy in an educative direction, we are creating a space for countless other habits and dispositions to take root. This, in many ways, is why having ideals and working to enact them in the present is so central to the work of educating. When we don't think about how the educational present of our students is developing habits of mind and heart that will have a great impact on the future, we leave far too much to chance; we don't achieve what is possible, and allow antidemocratic tendencies and anti-education sentiments in. In this light, the conclusion of the passage I quoted above becomes additionally important. Dewey writes, "What is native, spontaneous, and vital in mental reaction goes unused and untested, and the habits formed are such that these qualities become less and less available for public and avowed ends."

Here again Dewey's measured tone can keep us from seeing and feeling the weight that this line of thinking has for democracy and education. When students do not find channels for their energies in schools, they find other outlets and other audiences. Instead of feeling like a good and welcome contributor to the public life of school, they will begin to distrust the public space of school and seek private, and often disavowed, ends. Students may turn to the welcome arms of drugs and alcohol, of gangs, of hate groups online; or, the stakes may not be so dire, but equally detrimental to the public good: Instead of working toward our common stock of goodness, students may lose themselves in trivial gossip, trivial television, trivial habits.

What we must appreciate in this movement is that authority—as embodied by teachers and the school—is not seen as a trusted ally helping us all toward our common good. Instead, authority becomes something that must be subverted, distrusted, worked around. When this happens, democracy and education lose out. Think about how many in America relate to the idea of the government: It is a swamp that must be drained; it is bloated and out of touch; it is something that discredits and disparages the lives of black Americans; it is in the pocket of Wall Street. This large critique of government has roots—I would argue—in the way that many Americans experience school. Instead of school being a place where students feel supported and successful, school is a place where too many students learn that authority is impersonal, inefficient, uncaring, and falls short of its promises.

At the same time, just as there seems to be growing distrust of government, there is an equally pernicious growth of an ironic stance toward the very idea that we can make progress and collaboratively improve our common fate.[13] I would like to suggest that this stance might be tied to those who may have successfully played the game of school, but who have equally negative feelings about authority, because succeeding in school meant repressing one's actual interests instead of following them, and being rewarded for mere compliance and facility with gaming school instead of doing authentic and meaningful work. School fails both groups of students, because instead of school being a place where a student's present state of growth and interest were engaged and developed, students either learned to play the game of school and comply, had difficulty learning that game, or actively resisted it and so saw school as an inauthentic or inhospitable place.

This discussion of the game of school is meant to help us consider the ways in which the present created in our classrooms impacts the trajectory of a student's life. Are our classrooms spaces where students develop positive feelings toward authority because authority isn't arbitrary, or vengeful, or racist, or inauthentic and out of touch; do students see authority as that which facilitates growth that would be impossible absent that authority? Does authority—especially embodied in our system of public education—allow us to grow together toward our better selves and our better shared world? Or, does authority leave us distrustful, lesser selves, skeptical that anything can bring about positive social and personal change?

These are important questions for teachers and citizens of a democracy to ask. Is our democratic way of life creating the type of authority that facilitates positive personal and social growth? If not, what can be done? Though we can maintain a skeptical attitude toward the present state of our democracy in America, this skepticism should not lead to cool irony or passionate desire to tear the system down. Rather, we must see democracy as an experiment that lives in the quality of the present moment that we work to create. One tremendously important space for this experiment is in our educational institutions. Though policies and political mandates constrain and limit what can and cannot be done in schools, there is plenty of room to create more democratic relationships and more democratic spaces. From small acts, like letting students create their own classroom rules to larger acts of letting students manage discipline and punishment across the school, the goal is to show students that authority is not arbitrary or repressive, but capable of freeing potentials and possibilities. Students learn democracy in the present, and we need to provide opportunities for them to see that democracy isn't something waiting to happen, but a way of life they can experience in schools.

All this may sound terribly optimistic and is easy to disparage when large segments of the population seem to prefer authoritarianism and messianic supermen over truth, decency, and the collaborative hard work of making our world better. But, we cannot not let deviations from the ideal of democracy keep us from seeing the great wells of democracy (Marble, 2003) we can all still—and must—access in our lives. Dewey (2008h) tries to put the point as simply as possible in *Experience and Education* when he writes:

> I would ask a single question: Can we find any reason that does not ultimately come down to the belief that democratic social arrangements promote a better quality of human experience, one which is more widely accessible and enjoyed, than do non-democratic and anti-democratic forms of social life? Does not the principle of regard for individual freedom and for decency and kindliness of human relations come back in the end to the conviction that these things are tributary to a higher quality of experience on the part of a greater number than are methods of repression and coercion or force? Is it not the reason for our preference that we believe that mutual consultation and convictions reached through persuasion,

make possible a better quality of experience than can otherwise be provided on any wide scale? (LW.13.18)

Note here that Dewey is not making large claims that must be fulfilled by large external agents; here Dewey is describing democracy as a way of living we can all engage in. Listen to these words as a teacher. What does it mean to believe that "decency and kindliness of human relations come back in the end to the conviction that these things are tributary to a higher quality of experience on the part of a greater number than are methods of repression and coercion or force?" What does this look like in the classroom? Here is a place where practices need to come in line with our ideals and principles. If we believe in democracy—according to Dewey—we must treat our students with the type of decency and kindliness that leads to a higher quality of experience for those students in the present, so that they are fortified to make their future in collaboration with us and others, thereby building our common good.

Dewey goes on, "we believe that mutual consultation and convictions reached through persuasion, make possible a better quality of experience than can otherwise be provided on any wide scale." At root, this is why we teachers shouldn't force coercion through external or harsh measures; teachers enlist the interests and sympathies and ideals of students, thereby making the quality of our presents and our futures better. Our lives are improved through conversation and kindliness; though authoritarianism seems like a faster route to progress—just like *mere* preparation in education seems most efficient and expedient—we must return to what we all know at heart. The only lasting change for the better rests on the slow work of democracy. Though it may feel good to stand in front of a class of compliant children, this compliance comes at a great cost. We lose opportunities to grow in and through democracy. Here, again, we see why it is so important that we value the quality of the educational present we create and live in our classrooms, and do our all to experiment our way to more meaningful presents for our students.

I worry that this may sound all too idealistic, but I need to stress that we don't know what is possible until we make the effort to enact our ideals and assess the changing objective conditions that result because of it. As I mention in the introduction to this chapter, Dewey's thinking on ideals is far closer to what is presently called nonideal theory. In the next section I describe nonideal theory and discuss why it is important to understand that, for Dewey, ideals can always be revised in the face of facts (Fox & Westbrook, 1998) and we must experiment to realize our ideals; wishing or demanding are antithetical to their realization. Though we are driven by ideals, we know—we are reminded on an almost daily basis—that we live in a nonideal world, a world where democracy seems at risk and our present can feel far from educative or engaging. So, it can be easy to write Dewey off as idealistic, but to do so would be to give up on democracy and education far too easily.

## The Role of Ideals in a Nonideal World

Dewey believes in the ideal of democracy as a way of living, not just a form of government, and he believes that we cannot forgo educational opportunities in the present in the name of preparing students for a distant future that may never come. But, Dewey is not an idealist in the pejorative sense of the term. Rather, he is committed to experimenting to realize his ideals and he is committed to learning from these experiments and what they tell him about his ideals and the constraints of possibilities that arise as he experiments with his ideals. For Dewey, experimentation is continuous and ongoing, and we can never say of something as complex and evolving as democracy and education that we've realized the ideal. As we make progress toward the ideal, objective conditions change and new constraints and possibilities will arise. A great example of this can be found in Elizabeth Anderson's (2010) deeply important work on integration.

Anderson is committed to the ideal of integration on philosophical grounds, but she realizes that simply because integration is philosophically justified as an ideal, it does not mean that the goods of integration

will immediately appear once we break down legal barriers to segrega-
tion. As we experiment with integration, using busing and re-zoning,
for example, new constraints arise: massive resistance, white flight,
teacher attrition. Though new constraints arise, so too do new possibilities. Students and parents learn that every student can gain socially
and intellectually through integration and begin looking for ways to
expand this experiment or throw their faith more fully behind it. It is
hard to call integration a success or failure with anything approaching
certainty given the fact that our experiments in integration change the
objective conditions of school and society. As Anderson (2010) writes:

> Circumstances change, and new problems and complaints arise,
> requiring the construction of new ideals. If our ideals fail the test,
> we need to revise or replace them. This process is not merely instru-
> mental: it is not a matter of finding better means to a fixed end
> already fully articulated. Reflection on our experience can give rise
> to new conceptions of successful conduct. (pp. 6–7)

This is especially true with respect to integration, as reflections on
the history of schooling since the *Brown v Board of Education* decision
have shown, but I also think it is true when we think about making the
effort to break away from seeing education as preparation and seeing
education in terms of quality of the educational present. Following
Anderson's thinking, as we hold to the ideal of making the quality of
the educational present as meaningful as possible for our students, we
will work, for example, to create a more democratic space in our classrooms, where forced compliance is traded for persuasion and giving
students opportunities for self-direction that never existed for these
students before.

As we can imagine, especially if we've ever tried to make some
relatively major changes in our classrooms, students will respond to
any change, however minor, in expected and unexpected ways. Taking
the case of attempting to make our classrooms more democratic, some
students will invite and be prepared for more self-direction, others may
invite it but aren't fully ready for it in the way some of their peers are,

others may be ready for more responsibility but eschew it, and still others may resist any change as breaking the rules set forth in the game of school.[14] We can imagine more responses and many combinations of these types of responses. And, it can be easy to take what can feel like initial failure as a referendum on our ideals, but we must see the insight in Anderson's Dewey-inspired pragmatism: "it is not a matter of finding better means to a fixed end already fully articulated." We don't just implement means to a fixed end in classrooms; we experiment, open to possibilities that arise through the experimentation. If we believe in democracy, we see resistance to our ideals as a positive sign, a sign that what was once subterranean and hidden is now made publically available for conversation. More, this conversation can show students that views and ideals can be changed through conversation, and this process doesn't have to rely on coercion, power, or manipulation. Though these conversations can be difficult, and though students will need to learn how to engage in these types of conversations, these conversations are essential in a democracy.

One wonderful example of this can be found in Vivian Paley's (1993) *You Can't Say You Can't Play*. Paley wondered one day why it is that we allow young children to tell each other that they can't play. When we let children say "you can't play" we often create divides in the classroom, where there are children who play and children who almost always find themselves on the side of those who can't play. Paley thought this practice—though utterly commonplace—was not a decent or a kind one, and attempted to put an end to it by making one very simple rule in her classroom: You can't say, you can't play. No one in the class could utter those words, and Paley's book is the chronicle of the expected and unexpected results of this educational experiment based on her ideal that exclusion is something that should not be sanctioned by teachers. Paley found that many of the students who initially resisted the rule the most learned the most from it, and she found that the simple classroom experiment had far-reaching results that her students held with them into their futures. I bring this example up to show that something as common to the grammar of school as the practice of students telling each other that they cannot play is not something written—as it were—into the nature of school. Though it may feel natural, it is not fixed and set in stone; we can bring our ideals to the situation and fundamentally change the objective conditions of school that our students experience.

It is important to live in the realization that there is far more fluidity than fixity in our classrooms, and appreciate that we have space to work toward our educational goals and ideals. But, we must also realize that the fluidity cuts both ways. Just as we can use our ideals to reconstruct the worlds of our classrooms, the worlds of our classrooms—in their complexity and fluidity—should teach us that ideals aren't simply implemented: They are placed into a preexisting and ongoing conversation. That is—and to repeat—simply wanting something doesn't make it happen; what we hope for must find a welcome home with our students and within our classrooms. This takes work, work that should be informed by Dewey's (2008h) very helpful discussion from *Experience and Education*:

> It is no reflection upon the nutritive quality of beefsteak that it is not fed to infants. It is not an invidious reflection upon trigonometry that we do not teach it in the first or fifth grade of school. It is not the subject *per se* that is educative or that is conducive to growth . . . . There is no such thing as educational value in the abstract. (LW.13.27)

I hope this shows just how nonideological and responsive Dewey's thinking on education is. As Dewey writes, "There is no such thing as educational value in the abstract." It is not the case that there are "progressive methods" that are universally applicable across school contexts, and it is not the case that certain subjects or books are universally good or bad. What matters most is the quality of the interaction that a teacher facilitates between her students and the entire learning environment.[15]

To take my background as an English teacher as an example, there are absolutely times when classic literature is called for, but there are other times when engagement and interest can be cultivated by contemporary works or works specifically written for young adults.[16] One cannot approach teaching dogmatically—only classics, or classics are necessarily bad—one must do what is best for the particular students we are working with and given the short- and long-term goals we have for students. There is no formula for making the educational present as rich and meaningful as possible for our students, and so it is always useful to keep coming back to the idea that, "There is no such thing as educational value in the abstract." We keep revisiting our ideal of making the present engaging and empowering future learning, and we find materials and learning opportunities that help us realize that ideal, studying the impacts of what we do and creatively envisioning possibilities as the objective conditions of our classrooms change.

This approach to teaching is built upon interaction and not implementation. As Dewey helpfully points out: "The principle of interaction makes it clear that failure of adaptation of material to needs and capacities of individuals may cause an experience to be noneducative quite as much as failure of an individual to adapt himself to the material." Nothing is simple; eschewing simplicity and ideology we can only experiment with an eye toward continued growth. We must find what makes our material work—in the present—for our students, and cultivate those moments when the present is more like what we hope to live. As we keep that ideal of the most educative present in mind, we keep working—not abstractly, simplistically, ideologically—in the nonideal worlds of our classrooms to bring about more fully educative presents in the future. An important part of this process—and one not touched upon until just now—is the role that the past plays in our classrooms. An important aspect of learning from our classroom experiments is being in touch with the past: our past as an educator, the past our students have together and as individuals, and the immediate past that we share with our students. We cannot use a belief in the power of the present to keep us from seeing the impact that the past will play in our classrooms. Students come into our classrooms with a past, we come to our classrooms with a past, and the past—the very grammar of schooling—is very much with us in the present. These are things that cannot and should not be ignored, but we are also not *beholden* to the past; that is, the past—the past a student has had with education, our pasts as educators—is not our fate. To avoid making the past our fate, we must work to make the past come alive as a resource for learning in our present.

## Making the Past Available to the Present

Dewey routinely revisits the history of philosophy of education to draw out lessons for our educational present. He doesn't engage with the history of philosophy—be it Plato or Rousseau—in the hopes of finding solutions that can be applied to our educational present or because of their intrinsic value. Rather, Dewey engages with the past because he feels that it would be foolish for us not to engage with our educational history, in the form of works by philosophers of education, or as he hopes for future readers of *Schools of To-Morrow*, work done by educators attempting to realize their educational ideals (Dewey & Dewey, 2008). These are all resources we can draw on as we work to make our present as full as possible. But, they are only resources. Study of the past—be it study of the great works, or great achievements—is not something that has intrinsic value for Dewey, and Dewey is certainly not nostalgic; there is nothing to be made great again, instead there is only the open future to be achieved.

The achievements of the past are only there—and this is a very Emersonian thought[17]—to inspire future achievement. This is how Dewey (2008e) puts it in *Democracy and Education*:

> The present is not just something which comes after the past; much less something produced by it. It is what life is in leaving the past behind it. The study of past products will not help us understand the present, because the present is not due to the products, but to the life of which they were the products. A knowledge of the past and its heritage is of great significance when it enters into the present, but not otherwise. And the mistake of making the records and remains of the past the main material of education is that it cuts the vital connection of present and past, and tends to make the past a rival of the present and the present a more or less futile imitation of the past. (MW.9.81)

There is a lot in this short quotation that is worth taking up. To start, it is important to think through what Dewey means when he claims that "the present is not due to the products [of the past], but to the life of which they were the products." I mention above that Dewey's thinking on the past is very Emersonian, and here is what I mean by this. Emerson is frustrated that we revere books and not the *spirit* that went into the creation of the books. The book—according to Emerson—may inspire and educate, but if we are really interested in learning from a book, we must learn to appreciate the force behind the creation of the book; something like the creative or generative spirit. The accomplishment of Shakespeare in the form of something like *A Winter's Tale* is remarkable, but—according to Emerson—the play is nothing compared to the generative spirit that allowed for the creation of the play. One of Emerson's main messages for his readers is that our reverence of books and achievements of the past keeps us from accessing the generative spirit that leads to any and all creation. We should go to the past to gain a deeper appreciation of that spirit, and nothing more. Dewey doesn't use the language of spirit, but he does use the term *life* in the quote above. We learn from the past not through the products of the past, but through the "life of which they were the products." Previous attempts to make the present educative are important, but what is most important is that these attempts are examples of attempts dedicated to improving education, and it is the attempt—the drive to improve—that we should appreciate and seek to learn from.

One practical import of this understanding of our relationship to the past is that we learn to avoid making the past a rival to the present. We are not in competition, as it were, with Shakespeare; we are attempting to speak to our present in the spirit that Shakespeare beautifully cultivated to speak to his present. As well, because something wonderful was achieved in the past, it doesn't mean we can merely imitate it in our present. The world is in constant flux, and thinking we can pause time or reverse the course of time is a recipe for reactionary impulses that pull us away from reality. We need to fully engage with the present, using the example of the past as *inspiration* and not blueprint for the future.

It is important to note, as Dewey (2008h) does in *Experience and Education*, that living wholly in the present, *as if* the past did not exist, not only deprives us of inspiration that we need to respond creatively and intelligently—experimentally—to our present problems, but it also puts us in the position of not learning from the experiments of the past. The past exists and cannot be willed away. Injustices of the past live in the present;[18] fears that may have been an intelligent response to conditions of the past remain intact even though conditions change, and so arrests development. One cannot will or wish away nostalgia, bias, or habits developed through past experiences; the past lives on in the present and it can either be a spur or a curb to progress. What matters is how we *use* experience. Here is how Dewey (2008h) puts the point:

> The institutions and customs that exist in the present and that give rise to present social ills and dislocations did not arise overnight. They have a long history behind them. Attempt to deal with them simply on the basis of what is obvious in the present is bound to result in adoption of superficial measures which in the end will only render existing problems more acute and more difficult to solve. Policies framed simply upon the ground of knowledge of the present cut off from the past is the counterpart of heedless carelessness in individual conduct. The way out of scholastic systems that made the past an end in itself is to make acquaintance with the past a *means* of understanding the present. (LW.13.51–52).

We can see something like this in colorblind or history-blind approaches to combatting racism in school. Without adequate understanding of past injustices and how they live on in the present, we will only "render existing problems more acute and more difficult to solve." Knowledge of the past must be developed and cultivated as a *means* of understanding and responding to the present.

I hope we can see this quite clearly in the ways in which we interact with our own students in the classroom. Knowing something about a student's history with the subject I teach, with school more generally, with authority, and with frustration are important resources that I can use to teach. Making a child's past her fate or ignoring it with wishful thinking are both forms of mis-education that Dewey urges us to avoid. What we know about a child's past can be used to educate her more responsively (Gay, 2010); her past—her funds of knowledge (Moll, Amanti, Neff, & Gonzalez, 1992)—can be drawn on as we work to create the most educative present for her. To do this, we must be responsive—but not beholden—to her past.

A final important implication of Dewey's thinking on the past is to see that any accomplishment in the present must be overcome in the light of our open future. We never find success once and for all. Education and growth are a process of *becoming*.[19] As soon as we find some success in our educational present, objective conditions change: Students can do and expect more, and our next educational present must keep pace with this change or we risk being trapped into complacency by our past success, not working to make the present as meaningful as possible. This is something I find exhilarating as an educator, but I can see how it can be frustrating as well. That is, I often tell my students that if we take education seriously, we can never say that we are a good teacher: This is something that we are always in the process of becoming. Simply because I did something that worked well yesterday, or last year, doesn't guarantee or ensure that I will know what is needed tomorrow.

This is not to say that my past success does not matter, but it does mean that we must remain open to the learning and growth that needs to continue happening if we are to stay in touch with the generative spirit that creates the richest possible educational present. Methods and strategies are all very useful, but they are not guarantees; too much of the same and students don't continue growing and engaging. What we need is to remain in touch with the spirit of experimentation. A good life of teaching is not something achieved once and for all; it is something we are always in the process of living. New challenges will arise each year, some that we will struggle to respond to with the resources that we've developed in response to past challenges. What worked for past students might not work again in our present. Though this can feel frustrating, the fact that we must continue confronting challenges and changing landscapes means that we are always called to grow and learn. And, if we are committed to the life of education, knowing that we must always stand in a process of learning that offers no guarantee of future success, we can see this process of learning not as something frustrating, but a great gift we are given as educators, a gift that always keeps us close to the process of education because we are living it.

## Living Our Ideals: Life as an Experiment in Living

For Dewey, our lives in classrooms are best described as experiments in living.[20] We never achieve, with any kind of certainty, possession of the title "good teacher." Instead, we are always in process: We grow and develop our ideals and into our ideals, and we experiment and learn from our experiments of living those ideals. I think it is important to remember the Emersonian dimension of this approach to teaching, and recall Emerson's (1841/1983a) thinking in "Self-Reliance": "Life only avails, not the having lived. Power ceases in the instant of repose; it resides in the moment of transition from a past to a new state, in the shooting of the gulf, in the darting to an aim" (p. 271). Living the educational present is living in that transition state, the movement from repose and toward our educational aims.[21]

As I mention above, seeing the educational present as having the unique power of transition—I hope—makes it seem like the exhilarating educative state that it is, and not cause for frustration. Educators are under a great deal of pressure to "get things right," and for good reason: We are dealing with the ultimately important act of educating. But, the pressure to get things right can unduly narrow our aims, and it can cause us to shy away from a spirit of experimentation. Simply not messing things up can often crowd out our desire to take steps to make the classroom better. Sticking with the known—even though we know that it is not the state we want it to be—can feel like a safe bet, a bet that allows us to fall back on the idea that what we are doing works—as preparation, as helping students learn discipline—but when we think with Dewey, when we take his thinking on the educational present seriously, I hope we are inclined to see that we know that what we take to be "working" doesn't work to draw out the fullest potential from us, from our students, from our educational present.[22]

The key is not to beat ourselves up in the name of the ideal, but to hold the ideal as something we know is worth our energy and creativity. Other teachers are doing interesting things that we can learn from (Lewis & Hurd, 2011), resources are available that we can use to make our classroom more engaging (Morris & Hiebert, 2011), and we can focus less on our success and failure as an individual teacher and begin to see our work as tapping into the potential of teaching. When we move away from praise and blame of ourselves as individuals, when we see ourselves taking part in the work of teaching that we share as teachers, I hope it makes it easier to learn from and with others and that it becomes easier to take steps to change our practices. This is my hope, along with the reassurance that almost any move in the direction of our ideals—though it feels risky—is a step toward bringing about the present we want to live. It is not enough to want our classrooms to become better, and there is no magic that we could ever implement that will make our classrooms better. But, the passionate desire to bring about a richer educational present—for our students, for ourselves—coupled with the collaborative and creative spirit of experimentation, will help us live in the transition that is educative.

In the next chapter I discuss what happens to the self that lives in transition. That is, I look at what happens when we see education not as something that we achieve once and for all, but something that we are always in the process of living. Instead of teaching students that knowledge, skills, and understanding are things to be achieved, we can help students see what a life committed to learning looks like as an unending process of growth and development. We can stand as exemplars of being *that kind of self*, the self that is never content with past achievement, and always looking to stand in the moment of transition from the good to the better state. Living this way is the embodiment of living in the present. The past offers resources to draw on, and the future is an open possibility: What we do now, in the present, is what matters. Living in this present is what creates the self that is always in the process of becoming. This self will be the focus of the next chapter.

## CHAPTER 4

# We Make the Self by Living

Thinking about preparation is difficult, especially because—as teachers—we feel the weight of our responsibility to our students' futures. Our hope is that we empower our students to live better lives in the future, and we hope that there wasn't more that we could do to help make students' lives richer and more meaningful.[1] But, as Dewey stresses, we can't get lost in fear of what may come and so lose the present.[2] We make the best possible future for our students by creating an environment that allows them to live the best possible present.

This is the difficulty: We need to trust that a present that is engaging and educative will inspire our students to seek engaging and educative experiences in the future, and the experience of having the rich experiences we provided for them in the past will be the best preparation for creating and taking advantage of future experience.[3] Note that I use the word *trust* above. At its heart, education involves a great deal of trust. If a teacher doesn't trust the impossible potential of each student,[4] students won't learn to their fullest potential. If students don't trust their teachers, they won't gather all that the teacher offers. Though we may wish that we could get rid of this trust and push right to certainty, in the human act of educating, trust is central. So, though we may wish that we could find a type of preparation that guarantees our students the best possible future, this guarantee is not forthcoming. But, the desire for the guarantee can trouble the back of our minds; when we begin finding ourselves in the difficult world of experimenting toward ideals, someone who offers us more certainty can be very tempting. I hope we can avoid this temptation, and acknowledge that we live in the uncertain world of human education.[5] Education calls on our responsiveness to the potential we see in each of our students and the pedagogical imagination to create a present that draws this potential out and allows it to continue to grow in the future.[6]

It is complicated to see the germ of potential that must be cultivated in the present if it is to continue to grow into the future. It can be hard to see what differentiates this cultivation from mere preparation, but this is what my brief discussion of trust is meant to help us see. Seeing education as preparation is meant to give us confidence that we can trade some of the quality of the present for a promise of a better future. Dewey urges us not to take this trade, because loss of quality now will generally lead us to continue to compromise on what matters most: the quality of our experience. The issue is that when we get in the habit of deferring, or waiting, we see our better selves as something distant and to be achieved once and for all in the future instead of something that we must start working to realize now. We get in the habit of waiting for more ideal conditions before setting to work, instead of seeing the ways in which we can start that work in the nonideal conditions of the present.

Holding to a vision of the self as something to be achieved once and for all is problematic. I mentioned these examples briefly before, but I think they are worth repeating. For those of us who are academics, the process of becoming a tenured professor can be a confusing and hurtful one; it can lead to timidity and deferring. We tell ourselves that we will be able to do the work we want to do once we get tenure, but in those years of deferring, it may so happen that we lose touch with that which drove us to want to teach and study in the first place and so we don't become the type of selves we envisioned, even after we are granted tenure. Or, in other aspects of our lives, we can do similar things. Once I have a little more financial stability, I will do X. Once the kids are just a little older, we will be able to do Y. I will do this meaningless work now as preparing the grounds for security that will, at some point in the future, allow me to begin living.

I don't mean for this tone to be flippant or too knowing in its own way, and I understand that financial and other constraints can feel like fate. But, Dewey wants us to find a germ of hope in our ideals. If we can envision living differently, then we can begin finding ways to become the types of selves who live differently. There will never be ideal conditions to start this work, so we might as well begin now.

Another way to think about this question is to ask ourselves to think about how we *prepared* to do the types of things that we take joy in and that we would say we are good at. When we experience an excellent class, when our students all seem engaged and challenged, what prepared us for that? When we are hiking and feel absolutely lost in the present moment, what prepared us for that? When we find "flow" in any task—from cooking to accounting—what prepared us for that? While there are, no doubt, instrumental steps that allow us to take joy in the work that we do, I would also want us to see that our experiences of what our lives could be like also prepares us to do the work of living that life. That is, when we experience a moment of connection with a student when we are learning to teach, we get an intimation that this is the type of teaching we would like to do; the type of teacher we would like to become. When we plan a lesson that we would like to experience as a student, even if it doesn't go exactly as planned when we come to teach it, this helps us see the type of lesson designer we would like to become.

If I am onto something with this line of thought, I also hope it helps us think about our own students. Are we giving students opportunities to see themselves in the type of work we would like them to do now and in the future. That is, are we making them feel their way into the type of person who can speak Spanish well and enjoy and appreciate the varieties of Spanish-speaking cultures, or do they feel as if learning Spanish is a game they play in school, and one they aren't very good at? Is physical education something that is a daily embarrassment and a marker of a student's inadequacies, or something that gives them a glimpse of living a healthier and more fulfilling life?

I think many of us went into teaching because we love the subject that we teach and find something deeply important about it, but—when it comes to the way our students experience our classrooms—is this coming across? Are our students being merely prepared, or are they taking steps to become the type of self who has a life with poetry—for example—after they leave their formal education behind?

These questions, I feel, are important for teachers to ask and return to as they develop as educators. We should think about how we prepared to do the things we love to do now, and then think about how we might help students experience this type of preparation. When I think about my current work, writing and teaching, I feel like I am always in the process of doing both. I hear or read something and I think about how I might connect it to my teaching. I have an experience in my classroom or while preparing to teach, and it comes to me again while I am writing. Though it feels like I am always working in some way, this work never feels *obligatory*. This seems to be a key point that Dewey wants us to keep in mind.

If we are fully engaged with our work, questions of obligation and preparation are secondary to living as the type of person who does the work that we do. We never merely prepare to teach—though of course we are always preparing our classes, etc.—because as someone who lives teaching, we are always in the process of living as a teacher and so things like putting together activities for our students are part of who we are. I think it is important that we give our students a glimpse of this. The chemistry they are doing in our classes doesn't merely prepare them to do college-level chemistry, but it is an opportunity to see what it would be like to be a chemist or at least someone who appreciates and understands the role that chemistry plays in our world.

When we focus less on the distant end result, attaining a major in Chemistry or getting an advanced degree in the subject, and focus on living the subject, we are given another way to see what differentiates mere preparation from living in the fullness of the educational present. Living in the present allows us to approximate the self we would like to become by living and doing the type of work that that self will one day do more fully. It is not through mere preparation that we develop into that self; it is by living that self as best we can each moment that we develop into that the type of self we hope to become. As we learn to give better feedback and plan more engaging lessons, as we learn to be more responsive to students, we grow into *that* type of teacher;[7] the teacher who is always in the process of learning how to become her better teaching self and taking deeper joy in each educative interaction she has and facilitates.

## That Kind of Self

As I've been describing it, the Deweyan self is both something that is always in process *and* something that is an achievement. When we work toward our ideals, we are achieving, through approximation, our better selves, but a better self is not something that is gained once and for all. The self is made—and possibly unmade—each moment. We cannot claim that because we taught well once we are a good teacher; a good teacher is always in process: someone who lives as *that kind of teacher*. She develops into that teacher over time, and she grows into her work. If this is successful, then the line between things like self-interest and duty or obligation dissolve. That is, the teacher who spends extra time with each student does this work dutifully and responsibly, but she doesn't do it out of duty or a sense of responsibility.[8] Rather, she is interested—it is her interest as a teacher—to do good work, and this work will, by necessity, involve her taking responsibility for the quality of her interactions with each student. Dewey (2008e) makes this point in a long, but important, quote from *Democracy and Education*:

> Both sides assume that the self is a fixed and hence isolated quantity. As a consequence, there is a rigid dilemma between acting for an interest of the self and without interest. If the self is something fixed antecedent to action, then acting from interest means trying to get more in the way of possessions for the self—whether in the way of fame, approval of others, power over others, pecuniary profit, or

pleasure. Then the reaction from this view as a cynical depreciation of human nature leads to the view that men who act nobly act with no interest at all. Yet to an unbiased judgment it would appear plain that a man must be interested in what he is doing or he would not do it. A physician who continues to serve the sick in a plague at almost certain danger to his own life must be interested in the efficient performance of his profession—more interested in that than in the safety of his own bodily life. But it is distorting facts to say that this interest is merely a mask for an interest in something else which he gets by continuing his customary services—such as money or good repute or virtue; that it is only a means to an ulterior selfish end. The moment we recognize that the self is not something ready-made, but something in continuous formation through choice of action, the whole situation clears up. A man's interest in keeping at his work in spite of danger to life means that his self is found in that work; if he finally gave up, and preferred his personal safety or comfort, it would mean that he preferred to be that kind of a self. (MW.9.361)

There is a lot to this quotation, but—to start—it is important to see that it is set in motion by the criticism that human beings either act out of self-interest or selfless duty. In the context of teaching, this would mean that teachers are devoted to their work either because they are seeking some type of reward—more recognition, a better self-image—or out of selfless duty, the de-professionalizing narrative that teachers are, at heart, saints.[9]

Those in the first camp—the self-interest camp—believe that we improve teaching by offering the right types of external rewards—merit pay, teacher of the year awards—while those in the second camp—the selfless camp—are unable to appreciate that teachers don't pursue the work they love out of selfless duty, but because they find rewards internal to the work of teaching that are hard to appreciate and quantify if one doesn't have an appreciative understanding of something like the poetics of teaching (Hansen, 2004; Sherman, 2013). In Dewey's vision, a teacher doesn't work for money or fame, but this doesn't mean that she is selfless; that she doesn't take deep pleasure in her work or that teaching doesn't offer rewards that one must work carefully and diligently to realize. Here, as Dewey (2008h) does explicitly at the start of *Experience and Education* (LW.13.5), a dualism—the dualism of self-interest/selfless obligation—is reconstructed to make room for a more accurate picture of the world.

The self is not some fixed and isolated thing, it grows—or atrophies—in particular situations, through the *quality* of our efforts, interests, and ideals in those situations. In the case of Dewey's doctor, the doctor's self was formed in such a way that when faced with a plague situation, the doctor continued to be the type of self who serves. It is likely not the case that the doctor made a *calculated* decision—weighing the costs and benefits of continued service—but, instead, the doctor continued to serve because he was *that* type of self.

We can think about this in terms of teaching now as well. There are many times when students seem to call on more care and attention than we can muster, and yet don't give up in the face of these challenges. We seek our colleagues' advice, we experiment with new ways to reach the student, and we never give up, even though the situation seems intractable. We do this not because we are selfless or because we are seeking external reward; it is simply what we do as a teacher. We realize, even though we might not put it in Dewey's exact language, that "the self is not something ready-made, but something in continuous formation through choice of action." Simply having success with some students in the past is not enough to earn us the title of good teacher, nor is all lost given that we have not done what we take to be best by our students in the past. With each moment we have the chance to form the self through our choices of action.

It is important to attend closely to Dewey's language. As he writes, "A man's interest in keeping at his work in spite of danger to life means that his self is found in that work; if he finally gave up, and preferred his personal safety or comfort, it would mean that he preferred to be that kind of a self." Again, if we substitute teacher for doctor, a teacher can choose to give up on students who she fears will be too difficult—students who are too time consuming, or who seem overly resistant to instruction—but if she makes this choice, it is because she prefers to be that kind of teacher. Similarly, the new teacher who is told by teachers with more years teaching than her[10] that it is foolish or quixotic to believe that every student can learn and yet persists in holding this belief does so because she prefers to be that kind of teacher. Here, I want to be careful not to succumb to the sainthood myth I criticize above. Continuing to teach in the face of the challenges of classroom life is certainly not the same as doctoring in a plague situation, but the pressures teachers face on a daily basis are very real. Not only are teachers described as burning out, but Santoro (2011b) helpfully describes teachers as demoralized in the face of increased student testing. Teachers feel as if they cannot develop into the type of teacher they would like to become given high-stakes testing policy, and so would rather leave the profession than become *that* type of teacher.

What Santoro (2011a; 2011b) helps us see is that the moral dimensions of teaching are inseparable from the conditions in which one teaches. One's self is not something that can be abstracted and preserved; as Dewey reminds us, the self is "in continuous formation through choice of action." Our choices of action, and the constraints upon those choices given the environment we teach in, shape our selves. I think this realization can feel overwhelming, especially when teaching in environments that feel far from our ideals, but Dewey provides us with this vision of the self as a means to inspiring us to choose the better now, and not wait until we are confronted with the best, or hesitate in acting if conditions are not perfect.

By choosing the better, now, we begin becoming *that* type of teacher, the teacher who will persist in the face of difficulty because we prefer being that type of teacher. Note again, that this approach to teaching does not imply selflessness. Rather, this approach to teaching helps us realize that through the work of teaching we find that the "self is found in that work." To return to Hansen's (2004) thinking on the poetics of teaching, Hansen reminds us that there are countless rewards internal to the work of teaching. Seeing a student finally get a difficult concept, watching a student grow and mature over the course of a school year, feeling that one has taught a lesson that was simultaneously educative and engaging: These are the things that make teaching the tremendously rewarding work that it is.[11] Importantly, these are not abstract rewards—they are only achieved when we give ourselves over to our work. We find our teaching selves in the ways we respond to struggling students, we find our teaching selves in the ways we respond to policies we find mis-educative, and we find our teaching selves in the ways we practice self-care.

Each of these practices is ongoing, and as we grow into our practices, we find, like Dewey's doctor, that certain actions come to feel inevitable. That is, someone looking at how much work we put into student assessment, for example, may think that we are crazy. They may wonder: Why spend so much time on feedback, especially on a student who doesn't seem to "deserve" it, because the student probably will never become an exceptional student, and, what's worse, seems intent on testing the teacher at every turn? As teachers, we can see this as a flawed and external way of looking at the matter. Someone in the classroom sees that every student deserves our care and attention, and though much of our feedback may not trigger student growth, some of it will, and—for this reason—we keep at our work; we find ourselves in the work, and we find rewards through that work.

As I hope is clear, I think it is important to view excellence or goodness in teaching not as something that is achieved once and for all, but something that we live. Though this can feel frustrating, I think it is inspiring because it cuts against the myth that if we are not "natural born teachers" (Greene, 2014), then we are doomed to remain struggling teachers our entire careers.

Dewey reminds us that we can all grow into the profession of teaching. More, Dewey's vision reminds us that teaching, like all professions pursued through a moral lens, is a continuous adventure.[12] Teaching wouldn't be the rewarding work it is if it could be automated or made less uncertain through dehumanization. Because teaching is complex, moral work undertaken under the banner of uncertainty, it offers those of us who teach a chance for real adventure, because we take on our work in full acknowledgment that we aren't perfect and our best efforts can always be outdone.

Instead of feeling settled that we are good teachers, each day offers us a chance to become better, to grow more deeply into our work, to find rewards internal to teaching that we never knew existed. Again, there can be frustration in this uncertainty, and the distance we feel from our ideals can be overwhelming, but Dewey wants us to see that the self, formed through the continuous reconstruction of experience, empowers us to be unfazed in the face of challenges that can be described as impossible. This type of self does not need to decide to do ambitious and interesting work, as if the self were something external to the situation. The self, being *that* kind of self, does its work. Importantly, we never get to be this type of self by waiting for the perfect, or even the right, moment. We must begin the adventure, now.

## Deferring, Waiting, and the Loss of Self

Just as we teachers must begin the adventure of realizing our better selves, so too must we give this gift to our students. Our students should not be led to see school as a holding pattern, merely preparatory for doing interesting work in some distant future. Instead, we can take seriously the idea that the habits instilled by school can become our students' selves.[13] If our students are disengaged, restless, waiting for the opportunity to do something interesting, then they can become *that* kind of self: the self who lacks initiative, the self whose attention is superficial and divided, the self who is cynical, because the perfect time to finally begin acting seems further and further away.

This may be overstating the case or making an assumption based on limited experience, but when I work with first year college students, I am impressed by their openness, their dutifulness and their seriousness, but I often worry that my students aren't (yet) ready to take on the freedom of thinking, the adventure of college study.[14] I don't say this to blame my students or to make a judgment on their character or potential. I mention it because all the pressure that these students were under to be prepared for college, all of the hours spent in preparation that brought no immediate joy or benefit and the waiting to do "real work" in college has seemingly only produced students who have been prepared to wait: waiting for direction, waiting to be told what it means to do something interesting, waiting to finally start realizing who they are and what they care about within an academic setting.

As educators, we need to see this waiting, the deferring until some later date, as the real threat to education that it is. There will always be pressures that keep us from doing the work we want to do, and often these pressures will feel impossible. Though a common response to this pressure is to hope for better conditions, these conditions may never be forthcoming, and so we may find that we never get to do the work that we know we want to do. The only alternative, then, seems to be creating the future we have intimations of in whatever way we can now, in the present. This calls on tremendous pedagogical creativity, and it is deeply difficult to see how we are enacting our ideals in the very nonideal world of educational policy and practice that we live in.

As difficult as this work is, it should be heartening, because when we think seriously about what Dewey is asking of us, we can see a choice in front of us that we know the answer to already given the way it is framed. Dewey makes clear that we can choose to stay with the known that is not building toward the future we desire—telling ourselves all the while that this known is somehow *necessary* and preparatory, though we know this isn't the case—or we can choose to husband the moments we have, trying to bring about a small share of the better in each present moment we have.

To return to the example I give above of college students educated to wait, there are at least two responses to this reality. The first is to throw up one's hands and wish that students had a different type of preparation, and advocate for something like remedial classes for college students so that they can get the preparation they need to begin doing the ambitious, interesting, and creative work of college. This seems to be the approach that many colleges take.[15] An alternative approach, one based on Dewey's thinking on the present, is to begin the interesting work of college with students, knowing that the work won't look like what it would look like under more ideal circumstances. Though one may have to find different types of readings or learning activities under nonideal conditions, though one might have to creatively differentiate instruction, choosing to be the type of teacher who extracts the fullest educative significance of the present means that one is not extending the waiting pattern for students any longer.

Even though we choose to take the difficult step into uncertainty and experimentation, and even though we are left without the protective excuses provided by the language of preparation Dewey criticizes, we should take heart in the realization that we are finally freeing ourselves and our students to the present. Students, like the teacher, can now begin the adventure of extracting the educative potential of each moment.

Dewey makes this point across his collected work, but it is given a direct statement in *Moral Principles in Education*. Dewey (2008d) asks us to take very seriously the near impossibility of realizing our ideals when we hold onto a misguided vision of preparation. He writes:

> The school cannot be a preparation for social life excepting as it reproduces, within itself, typical conditions of social life. At present it is largely engaged in the futile task of Sisyphus. It is endeavoring to form habits in children for use in a social life which, it would almost seem, is carefully and purposely kept away from vital contact with the child undergoing training. The only way to prepare for social life is to engage in social life. To form habits of social usefulness and serviceableness apart from any direct social need and motive, apart from any existing social situation, is, to the letter, teaching the child to swim by going through motions outside of the water. (MW.4.272)

Though the sentiments Dewey expresses in this quotation are well-known, within the context of our thinking about the educational present, I hope they take on renewed significance. As Dewey writes, the school "is endeavoring to form habits in children for use in a social life which, it would almost seem, is carefully and purposely kept away from vital contact with the child undergoing training. The only way to prepare for social life is to engage in social life." Here I want to start at the smallest possible scale of change and reconstruction, at the level of the teacher working with her students in the classroom. That is, instead of waiting for the entire educational system, or the school district, to embrace deeper, more meaningful learning, I want us to consider what it would mean for the teacher to create "habits in children for use in a social life" that are deeply engaged, engaging, and democratic.

Here—again, starting small and simply—I wonder if teachers could make it a part of their pedagogical practice to check in—at the end of the day or week or unit of study—and ask the simple question: How are my students doing in terms of the *habits* they are developing in my class? Are students feeling more confident and open to critique? Are students feeling like they belong in the classroom and that they can articulate their fears, frustrations, and hopes with the teacher and their peers? Are there procedures in place where students find a voice and a community?

These are only a few of the questions that we might make part of a pedagogical practice that grounds us in the present while thinking about how the present ways of being in my classroom impact the habits that will carry a student and sustain, or constrain, her in her future inside and outside of school. When students feel less than, that they don't belong, that there is no way for their voice to be heard and valued, how will this influence the student's future? To take a brief, if negative, example, my daughter was in an elementary classroom where the teacher makes a point of punishing the entire class for the behavior of a few students. She makes a scene of calling attention to the misbehaving students and subtly—or maybe not so subtly, since my daughter knows exactly what is going on—asking for peer pressure, if not outright shunning, as a means to getting the misbehaving ones to comply. While this type of classroom management strategy is no doubt common, and though it probably has the so-called wisdom of practice behind it[16]—we need to be mindful what these practices accomplish and what habits they set in place. My daughter—and I don't think she is unique in her reaction—has come to, in a minor but still troubling way, distrust authority as arbitrary and has wondered about the place of personal responsibility—her own, not that of the other students—in a world where she can be punished for something she did not do and could not really even conceive of doing.

More, it should be easy to imagine what happens to the "noncompliant" students in this classroom environment: If they were seeking attention, they got more of it, even if it was mis-educative attention; they don't have the opportunity to build a restorative relationship with the teacher and the classroom community; they begin to inhabit the role of the "bad" student or the "problem child" and this role is publicly assented to by the authority of the teacher and the pressure of the peer community.

It is easy to be dismissive of this line of thinking as an overinvolved or overthinking parent who doesn't know what it is like to try to effectively educate and manage a group of twenty elementary schoolers. And, though I would like to think I am open to criticism on any number of fronts, when it comes to using the power of the teaching role in ways that seem to undermine the development of healthy community and healthy self-regulation on the part of students, I think it is important to see that we can do both; that teachers regularly have orderly classroom environments that don't have the potential to put in place long-term mis-educative habits in students.

Or, to make the positive case, something important happens when a teacher disrupts the habit of anointing winners and losers in the classroom. When, through her example and manner (Fenstermacher, 2001), the teacher takes every student seriously, regardless of the student's facility with the subject, her expressed interest (or lack thereof), or her history as a student, new possibilities emerge in the classroom. Not only will the lives of the students who are treated with a more inclusive regard develop new habits, but students who feel pressured to perform to an external standard, to win the game of school, develop different ways of thinking about their identity and other students. Instead of seeing the classroom and the school as a place of contest, a zero-sum game where some must win and some must lose (Labaree, 2012), the students and the teacher will see new possibilities for school, and society. Habits formed in a classroom where students understand that "fair isn't always equal" (Wormeli, 2006) will be quite different from habits formed in a classroom where every student is punished for the behavior of a few students.

The point of these examples is to remind us teachers of the importance of taking what Dewey (2008h) calls the "long look ahead" (LW.13.50). Though our approach to management may win short-term compliance, what happens to our students when they go home or leave our classrooms? Asking these types of questions are what I would like to call a pedagogical exercise. That is, like a spiritual practice like mindfulness or a spiritual exercise in the Ignatian (Martin, 2012) or philosophical tradition (Hadot, 1995), the act of trying to discern the long-term impact of the work done in the present with students may not provide clear, direct, or immediate guidance, but the very practice of considering the questions of the present's impact on the future will prove transformative.[17]

When we consider the quality of a student's present as a way of thinking about her future, we will begin to both be more attentive to the present well-being of students and begin transforming our relationship to education as preparation. Instead of mindlessly filing an activity into the bin of the preparatory as a means of justifying its use, we can take the broader view, and consider what impact the explicit and hidden curriculum might have on the habits our students are developing. As we continue living these questions (Gordon, 2007), we, as teachers, will develop habits of noticing that may allow us to reconstruct and reevaluate the way that time works in our classrooms, giving us the courage to focus less on work that appears preparatory but does not prepare, and focus more on experimenting with activities that may prove more educative and sustaining in the long run. Again, these pedagogical exercises will not give us sure paths forward, but the very practice of looking at ours classroom through the lens of Dewey's "long look ahead" will work wonders on the pedagogical imagination, illuminating possibilities where before we could only see constraints and the well-worn path that was not leading to the present or futures we hoped to live when we embarked on the work of teaching.

## Reconstructing Preparation

As our experience with these types of pedagogical practices deepens, informing our pedagogical imagination and the experiments we undertake in our classrooms, we begin to move farther away from education as mere preparation and toward a deeper appreciation for what it means to cultivate a quality present as the only way to ensure a more fully educative future. As an aid to deepening these pedagogical practices, passages from Dewey are often deeply instructive. To see how this might be the case, I turn our attention to a long passage from Dewey's (2008e) *Democracy and Education* where he asks us to reflect on what it means to really fortify a student for a more educative future. The full quote runs MW.9.320–321, but I will break it into smaller pieces and reflect with it as a means to modeling the pedagogical exercises I suggest above. Dewey begins,

> The only adequate training *for* occupations is training *through* occupations. The principle stated early in this book (see Chapter 6) that the educative process is its own end, and that the only sufficient preparation for later responsibilities comes by making the most of immediately present life, applies in full force to the vocational phases of education. The dominant vocation of all human beings at all times is living—intellectual and moral growth. In childhood and youth, with their relative freedom from economic stress, this fact is naked and unconcealed. To predetermine some future occupation for which education is to be a strict preparation is to injure the possibilities of present development and thereby to reduce the adequacy of preparation for a future right employment. (MW.9.320)

As I read this passage, I find the important repeated theme of preparation reiterated, but my thought goes to the middle sentence: "The dominant vocation of all human beings at all times is living—intellectual and moral growth." Here is a line that we can repeat in our minds, so that we spend time with it and let it slowly grow in its significance for our practice as educators. As French teachers, or math teachers, or coaches our immediate goal is teaching our students how to conjugate irregular verbs, or find the area under a curve, or release the discus for its best flight. But, though this is our immediate goal, we have to remember that, through all of this, each student is first and foremost a human being, whose dominant vocation is intellectual and moral growth.

Again, think about the subjects we teach and the students we teach these subjects to. How often are we able to stop and remember that as deeply important as our subject is, the *dominant vocation* of the students we work with is intellectual and moral growth? If the answer is not often, or not often enough, Dewey would urge the pedagogical exercise of stopping and thinking this through. If we are at the stage of thinking about this, Dewey would ask that we take the steps to experiment with what it would mean to teach with this at the front of our planning, our bearing, and the ways in which we interact with students. As I've stressed, this thinking doesn't issue forth in exact guides to practice, but it does lead to changing our relationship to those practices.

For example, when we see that the dominant vocation of each of our students is their general intellectual and moral growth, we may find that we are more patient when students don't make our subject the center of their world. If this proves difficult or frustrating, then we may also begin to find new ways to make our subject relevant to their pressing intellectual and moral concerns. Not as a way of cheapening our subject to make it "relevant," but because we want to offer an invitation to thinking that our students will take an interest in, and that does justice to the subject we care deeply enough about to teach.

More, Dewey gives us resources to quiet the voice that wants to tell us: "But, they won't be prepared if you change your practices . . ." We quiet this voice by remembering the reality that our students will be employed because they have certain skills, but often also because they are a certain type of person. That is, as important as it is to know how to do what is required at a certain job, it is often more important, especially given how quickly most fields are changing, that we are the type of person who sees continuous growth as an exciting possibility and not a threat.

If we teach students to be open to the new, to take pleasure in growing intellectually and morally, how can they not but be prepared to do good work, even if they may have to Google some facts from time to time in order to do their work or watch quick videos to learn needed skills. This may be simplistic, but I hope it has something of a ring of realism, if not truth, to it. Dewey goes on:

> To repeat the principle we have had occasion to appeal to so often, such training *may* develop a machine-like skill in routine lines (it is far from being sure to do so, since it may develop distaste, aversion,

and carelessness), but it will be at the expense of those qualities of alert observation and coherent and ingenious planning which make an occupation intellectually rewarding. In an autocratically managed society, it is often a conscious object to prevent the development of freedom and responsibility; a few do the planning and ordering, the others follow directions and are deliberately confined to narrow and prescribed channels of endeavor. However much such a scheme may inure to the prestige and profit of a class, it is evident that it limits the development of the subject class; hardens and confines the opportunities for learning through experience of the master class, and in both ways hampers the life of the society as a whole. (MW.9.320)

Education that trains for machine-like skill is unduly limiting, and it "hampers the life of the society as a whole." Here too, is cause to reflect. If we agree that democracy is preferable to autocracy, and if we further believe that the jobs of the future will be less and less machine-like (given the fact that machines can do these jobs much better than we can [Davidow & Malone, 2014]), then why would we think that *mere* preparation—in the sense of drilling students to do low-level thinking through routine and memorization—will be a fitting education? It only seems to make sense that we would seek to educate the whole child (Noddings, 2005) and embrace calls for deeper learning aimed at developing 21st century skills (Martinez & McGrath, 2014).

As we consider this, as our minds wander to objections and difficulties of practice, we may recall Dewey's admonition that "the dominant vocation of all human beings at all times is living—intellectual and moral growth." Whatever the jobs of the future look like, our students will always be developing intellectually and morally, and our classrooms can either make this development broader, deeper, more engaging, or slow and narrow that development by channeling it into activities that don't call for a moral or an intellectual response: activities that call for mere mechanical skill or narrow tasks that don't call on our whole minds and our whole selves. Dewey continues,

The only alternative is that all the earlier preparation for vocations be indirect rather than direct; namely, through engaging in those active occupations which are indicated by the needs and interests of the pupil at the time. Only in this way can there be on the part of the educator and of the one educated a genuine discovery of personal aptitudes so that the proper choice of a specialized pursuit in later life may be indicated. (MW.9.320)

Dewey's use of indirect in this quotation reminds me of one of the great lines from *Democracy and Education*, where Dewey (2008e) reminds educators that "frontal attacks are even more wasteful in learning than in war" (MW.9.176). Education—for Dewey—is finding the delicate balance between order and disorder; freedom for the student and direction provided by the educator.

While ignoring a student's future as a wage-earner and member of society is neglectful, a direct focus on future occupations will likely unduly limit how a child grows into her future. The trick, and a difficult one, is to allow students to experience the "*genuine* discovery of personal aptitudes." Here, especially, one may wish for more direct guidance from Dewey, but the reminder that students do have genuine and personal aptitudes is enough to help me put the brakes on a train of thought that would like to fit a young person to a career, or a graduate program, before allowing the student the proper time to experience success in a variety of fields so that she has a better sense for her calling. What this will look like for different students, in different fields of studies and at different stages of their development, will of course differ. But, the key point is to create an educational present where students experience the "*genuine* discovery of personal aptitudes" so that they might be better able to make a more educated choice as to specialized pursuit later in life.

As important, even once the choice of field or career is chosen, it most certainly doesn't mean that the process of growth ends or is wholly circumscribed by that chosen field. Remember: "The dominant vocation of all human beings at all times is living—intellectual and moral growth." So, even though we have chosen the profession of teaching, this does not mean that all our intelligence, our entire sense of our selves are found in that work. Our intellectual and moral growth continue in other fields, and certainly inform our teaching selves and the work we do in our classrooms. But, if we narrowly conceived of our lives as preparation for teaching, or under the obligation of the profession of teaching, we would cease to grow and develop into the best possible teachers. The quotation from *Democracy and Education* we are considering continues:

> Moreover, the discovery of capacity and aptitude will be a *constant* process as long as growth continues. It is a conventional and arbitrary view which assumes that discovery of the work to be chosen for adult life is made once for all at some particular date. One has discovered in himself, say, an interest, intellectual and social, in the things which have to do with engineering and has decided to make that his calling. At most, this only blocks out in outline the field in which further growth is to be directed. (MW.9.320–321)

I value this line of thinking as a reminder and an admonition. Once we find a passion for something, we are invited to a *constant* process of discovery. This is a beautiful way of thinking about vocation, especially the call to teach. It is not as if we learn, once and for all, how to teach and who we are as teachers. Instead, "the discovery of capacity and aptitude" is something that we are engaged with, "a *constant* process as long as growth continues."

As a pedagogical exercise, we can read and return to this line any time we are feeling stuck or lost in the details of our work. We did not become teachers to do work that could be mechanized, and so when we begin developing thoughtless or mechanized responses to students and their work, it is time to take a moment and reconnect with the possibilities for growth and change that are a part of any profession.

More, Dewey's thinking is an admonition to not only turn against the mechanized—what the poet W. H. Auden calls the "rehearsed response"[18]—but to actively cultivate a desire for intellectual and moral growth in its many forms. To take what might seem like an example found in absurdist art, can we ever imagine a teacher whose only reading is professional work on teaching and her field, and who only views films about the profession and will only attend speaker events and workshops that are on teaching or her field? Or, can we imagine a teacher teaching effectively based solely on her experience in teacher education and with professional literature? I doubt we can, because we know that teaching calls on our entire selves. Our professional training and continuing education, while no doubt necessary, is also in no way sufficient for the multifaceted work of teaching. Dewey wants us to be mindful so that we do not come to believe that the "discovery of the work to be chosen for adult life is made once for all at some particular date," but see that as we mature and gain new life experiences, what it means to inhabit living teaching will likewise develop, expand, and grow.

At the same time, as we broaden our own understanding of what it means to grow into and through living and teaching, we can see that we must reconceive what it means to prepare students for the future. Just as it is—at least for me—hard to imagine an excellent teacher who only reads professional literature, I find it hard to see how we can develop students who are passionate about our subject areas if they only engage with material created for school: textbooks, instructional videos, and standardized tests. As Daniels and Zemelman (2014) remind us within the context of content area reading, very few adults will ever pick up a textbook to learn about something they are developing a passion for. If this is the case, why do we feel as if textbooks, and other material created for school, will be enough to prepare a student to grow into a lifelong passion for our subject area?

As I've stressed, these questions are meant to be provocations, not opportunities for me to "solve" the problems of practice and certainly not meant as judgments of other teachers and their classrooms. The provocation here is to take seriously the ideal of growth, and consider what types of experiences and environments will best promote growth and habits that will lead to continued growth in the future. A group of teachers talking about their classroom, or forming a book club on material seemingly unrelated to the day-to-day work of teaching, may do more to promote growth than any narrowly tailored in-service training can ever hope to accomplish. If this suggestion sounds reasonable, then the hope is that we can begin to discern *what* preparatory work is effective, and what is preparatory only in name.

Given the openness of our growth into and through a profession, it is useful that Dewey reminds us that our choice to become a teacher does not set us unto a narrow road, but it offers a broad vista, a "field in which further growth is to be directed." Dewey continues,

> It is a sort of rough sketch map for use in direction of further activities. It is the discovery of a profession in the sense in which Columbus discovered America when he touched its shores. Future explorations of an indefinitely more detailed and extensive sort remain to be made. When educators conceive vocational guidance as something which leads up to a definitive, irretrievable, and complete choice, both education and the chosen vocation are likely to be rigid, hampering further growth. In so far, the calling chosen will be such as to leave the person concerned in a permanently subordinate position, executing the intelligence of others who have a calling which permits more flexible play and readjustment. And while ordinary usages of language may not justify terming a flexible attitude of readjustment a choice of a new and further calling, it is such in effect. If even adults have to be on the lookout to see that their calling does not shut down on them and fossilize them, educators must certainly be careful that the vocational preparation of youth is such as to engage them in a continuous reorganization of aims and methods. (MW.9.321)

Here is another place where I love Dewey's language, in particular the phrasing of the attitude of desiring growth as allowing for: "more flexible play and readjustment." This is a wonderful sentiment, particularly as it relates to teaching. While teachers often feel, are explicitly made to feel, as if they are consigned to a "subordinate position, executing the intelligence of others," Dewey reminds us in this passage that even the most narrowly vocational jobs allow for flexible play and readjustment. How much more so when considering the life of teaching? As constraining as policies, local ways of doing things, and opinions of parents and administrators can feel, Dewey wants us to relish the "flexible play" that exists along with the possibilities of readjustment. As fixed as our reality feels, we are not fossilized: to be human is to be able to grow morally and intellectually.

We have to recognize this ideal of growth as an ideal, especially when countless pressures aim to narrow the work of teaching to the implanting of information into children that is then reproduced on a standardized test. Coupled with this, Dewey reminds us of the pressure internal to teaching, and one that teachers may have more control over. He writes, "If even adults have to be on the lookout to see that their calling does not shut down on them and fossilize them, educators must certainly be careful that the vocational preparation of youth is such as to engage them in a continuous reorganization of aims and methods." Even before the current push for accountability through standardized testing, we should wonder how good we were, as individual teachers and as a profession, at not fossilizing students and instead freeing them for meaningful growth and development.

This statement can sound like a judgment, but it is meant as a provocation, an invitation to thought. How, either intentionally or unknowingly, have we constrained a student's future growth by the quality of the present we create in the classroom, and how have we set students on the path to deeper learning? Dewey's extended quotation we considered in this section leads to this question, and as a model of what I am suggesting as a pedagogical exercise, I hope it helps us take stock of where we stand, and allows us to un-settle habitual and habituated action and work to create new habits that are more educative, that allow us to continue to grow morally and intellectually.

Living can become merely routine, and our lives driven by habits that narrow our vision and limit our possibilities. By contrast, we can form habits that are the embodiment of our ideals, leading us to see life and the process of living as an invitation to further growth. Growth and habit are key terms for Dewey, and for the teacher they need to become a matter of reflection-in-action (Munby, 1989; Rodgers, 2002). That is, the teacher needs to think through the roles that habits play in her classroom and how the habits formed in her classroom make possible, or constrain, future growth. The pedagogical exercise of reading Dewey is one that encourages our own growth as educators, and can empower us to take the risk of breaking with habituated modes of operating in pursuit of a more educative present that frees our students to see being alive as an opportunity for continued growth.

## Where Do We Find Ourselves?

The title of this section comes from the first sentence of Emerson's (1844/1983b) wonderful essay "Experience," and I use it here to re-sound Emerson's distinctive call—one taken up by Dewey—to do the work of creating our better selves and our better world. To do this work, though, we must look soberly, but not cynically, at where we stand. Only when we undergo pedagogical exercises that force us to confront the limitations of our current classrooms can we take it upon ourselves to remake our classrooms and become the type of teachers who facilitate a quality educational present for their students. Becoming *that* type of teacher takes work and pedagogical creativity, but Dewey's vision of the self is inspiring because it is not fatalistic and it is not reliant on the magical thinking that paralyzes us from acting in anything but ideal conditions.

Dewey gives us courage to act in the nonideal condition of our world, though he does ask that we recognize that we are responsible for working to create the self we want to live in accordance with ideals that we find inspiring. We don't need ideal conditions to start this work, because we have to recognize that our selves, like it or not, are made and remade, constructed and reconstructed by the quality and depth of the life they experience. It is the quality of our presents that form the people we are. It is through the full scope of living that we are perpetually becoming our selves. Though desiring or intending to be a certain type of teacher is undoubtedly important, how we enact and live those desires and intentions is what matters. It is the habits we form and the experiences that those habits either foreclose or make possible that form who we are. Everything we do and intend combines to make us *that* kind of self and no other.

Holding onto ideals, practicing pedagogical exercises, and reading texts like Dewey all allow us to take steps toward unsettling what has become fossilized, but the step to action is also important. Here is how Dewey (2008h) puts it in *Experience and Education*:

> A professional businessman wishes to succeed in his career; a general wishes to win the battle; a parent to have a comfortable home for his family, and to educate his children, and so on indefinitely. The intensity of the desire measures the strength of the efforts that will be put forth. But the wishes are empty castles in the air unless they are translated into the means by which they may be realized. The question of how soon or of means takes the place of a projected imaginative end, and, since means are objective, they have to be studied and understood if a genuine purpose is to be formed. (LW.13.45–46)

We desire to be good teachers, and the *intensity* of that desire should correlate to the "strength of the efforts that will be put forth." The stronger our intention and desire, the greater strength we can muster for their realization. Pedagogical exercises where we develop an intention are necessary, because they help us realize that we have the strength to act. Importantly, once we realize the need for action, we also realize that we work in the realm of the imperfect, and so we must study and reflect and compromise as we find ways to become the self we envision within the conditions we find ourselves in.

The interconnection between desire, effort, and imperfect means is the basis of selfhood. Lacking desire or not putting forth enough effort or wishing the world would be different or immediately amenable to our will causes us to become one type of self. Taking heart, putting in effort we didn't know we were capable of, and seeing possibilities where others see fixity cause us to become another self altogether. Dewey urges us to become the second type of self, like the doctor who persists in her work because she cannot imagine being anything but that self.

Though we cannot change the past or the conditions we find ourselves in, we can change the way we view those conditions, and we can choose to take the first step in approximating our ideals in the very real and messy world we live in. Once we take that first step, new possibilities and challenges will emerge, calling us to respond in ways we cannot foresee. But, taking that first step, envisioning possibilities where all we saw before was fate, is the only preparation we need to take the next step, and the next. As we begin this journey, as we make the self by walking in this way, we can see even more clearly what Dewey hopes for students, because we will be living this education and growth for ourselves. Instead of waiting, we will start building the present we want to live. We will lose patience with the merely preparatory because we will know what it means to extract meaning and life from the present. Patience lost, we will make the attempt to create the types of learning environments that allow students the opportunity to experience the new life of growth that should be the aim of any form of education worthy of the name.

# Futures for the Present

The experiment of American democracy is ongoing and always at risk. This fact, the fact that America is an experiment, and an experiment that is not predestined to be successful, is easy to miss given some of America's other promises: the promise of opportunity, the promise of the American Dream, the promise that anyone who works hard will be handsomely rewarded. At times of relative prosperity for large numbers of (white) Americans, America can feel fully settled, settled in the belief that America is great, and that those who are advocating for more—rights for black and brown Americans, LGBTQ rights, rights to question American interventions around the world or America's moral standing in relation to its own ideals—are somehow ungrateful. Or, at times of great doubt and uncertainty—America's involvement in the Vietnam and more recent wars, America's failure to address or even recognize our changing climate, the wide circulation of videos showing police shootings of unarmed black men—it can feel as if the experiment of America and the ideals behind that experiment are little more than a thin cover for American violence, colonialism, and injustice. Between cynicism about the very possibility of America and its ideals and nostalgia for a time when America was once great stands our present moment.

In this chapter I investigate recent controversies on college campuses as a means to think about the types of education that are needed in our K–12 schools. I do this for a few reasons. First, considering the lives of college students in our present age helps us consider what type of educational presents they need in high school in order to navigate their educational presents in college. Second, the very idea of the good of college education seems to be under attack. According to a 2017 Pew survey, only 43% of Republicans view higher education in a favorable light, while 37% view it negatively (this is an 11% downturn of positive feelings and an 8% uptick in negative feelings in just two years). When we consider this in relation to the concerted effort to delegitimize the veracity of established news outlets like the *New York Times*, one needn't be an alarmist to be deeply worried about the state of our democracy when rigorous scholarship or well-researched news articles are denigrated and devalued and trumped by, or replaced with, hate speech and conspiracy theory (Muirhead & Rosenblum, 2018). With this radical revaluation of values, we must recognize that our youth is deeply confused. Standards of conduct, standards of evidence, standards of decency, and much else have been overturned, and it is unclear, at present, what they are being replaced with. Again, I don't think it behooves us to be alarmist, but we have to wonder what is being undermined, if not outright destroyed, in our present and what our youth will be left with: what standards to emulate, what goods to hope for, what models of virtue to strive for.[1]

It is with this background that I turn to events that transpired on the Middlebury College campus on March 2, 2017.[2] Students at Middlebury College, confused about the state of our country after the election of Donald Trump,[3] were further confused when it seemed that their College would at least tacitly endorse[4] someone like Charles Murray who is labeled as an apologist for white supremacy in some quarters.[5] Though what happened at Middlebury, as it devolved into violence and deep incivility, is inexcusable behavior, the backlash seems irresponsible as well. In the rush to make this event about free speech, the hypocrisy of liberals who don't tolerate ideas they don't agree with, and a generation of young people who are variously described as snowflakes or violent members of an un-thinking mob, we fail to see what *educational* value there is in inviting so-called controversial speakers to college campuses, especially small private liberal arts colleges whose unique mission is to help students recognize and appreciate excellence in all its forms so that they can become creators of this type of work.[6]

In connection to Dewey's thinking on preparation and the quality of the educational present, I focus on the specifically educational value of controversial speakers, granting that I am in no way claiming comprehensive coverage of this issue.[7] Middlebury College attracts and accepts some of the best high school students in America, and so the events at Middlebury should cause us to ask questions about the quality of their preparation to become active participants in democratic life. Though many of these students, no doubt, scored 5s on multiple AP tests and scored close to perfect if not perfect on their SATs, when they were confronted with a situation that left them in a moral quandary, they responded in ways that left large segments of the American population, across the political spectrum, troubled.

While it is easy to look for scapegoats—professors who are tenured radicals, students who are snowflakes, colleges that claim to value diversity and yet don't allow for a diversity of opinion on campus—it may be more instructive to consider the preparation these students had, before Middlebury, asking ourselves the question: What could their education before Middlebury have done to prepare them for this situation? When we think that many of these young people—just months before—would have had to ask permission to go to the bathroom, and would have had their life controlled by bells that shuffled them between fifty minute periods that culminated in a battery of standardized tests, we might feel a little less self-righteous shock and take a little more interest in the quality of the education these young men and women received leading up to this incident.

Instead of making this event at Middlebury revolve around free speech and the silencing of Murray and other campus speakers, we can also take this as an opportunity to look at how secondary education in this country prepares students for what it means to be responsible agents in our experiment in democracy.

While personal responsibility is deeply important, this is something that one must be educated into, and not something that should be assumed simply because one is of age and on a college campus. More, it is worth wondering if the desire to protest on the part of many Middlebury students came from a desire to create harm or to silence Murray, or from something like a desire to do the right thing. This may be hard to appreciate, especially as these protests devolved into violence. But, I am struck—with the college students I have the good fortune to work with—by the earnestness and desire to do the right thing I sense when working with them. These students want to save our environment, they want to advocate for people they feel have been wronged, and they want to become better people. So, if we see these students as genuinely motivated to do the right thing, and if these students are told, or hear, that their college is inviting someone to campus who is a proponent of racist thinking, I hope we can appreciate why these students may respond with a sense of moral outrage and a desire to set the scales of justice right.

Here is the important part. I think colleges like Middlebury—and the K–12 schools preparing students for college—need to begin anticipating this outrage *and* educate that outrage into channels that do not result in violence.[8] This strikes me as one of the most difficult aspects of our current political moment, and one that is lost in the effort to vilify students and higher education institutions. Easy vilification doesn't allow us to appreciate how student outrage may be coming from a morally justified place, even when it issues forth in morally unjustifiable, or at least morally questionable, actions. Instead of focusing on how schools can channel justified outrage, we are blaming students for the education in responsibility we've failed to provide them with.[9]

I worry that in the rush to vilify college students and colleges we almost wholly ignore what can be learned from this experience. I interpret the events at Middlebury College—as a Middlebury graduate and professor at a small liberal arts college[10]—as an example of how adults are passing the buck back to students who have not been prepared—and are not being prepared—to actively engage with the experiment that is American democracy. These students are not necessarily malicious; in fact, I find my students to be of a great good will and actively searching for guidance on issues that matter. They desire an education that will fit them for productive, moral, engaged democratic life, and we seem incapable of providing them with this education. We tell them about the importance of conforming to our demands so that they might be prepared for college, but we do not provide them with an education that allows them to use their moral outrage to address the problems of our present.

Providing students with this type of education has been a major concern of this book, and I turn to a few passages from Dewey as a way charging us with taking responsibility for the quality of the educational presents our students experience so that we may revitalize American democracy in our time. Neither cynical nor nostalgic, I believe, with Dewey, in the pragmatic hope that we can become better than we are. Not through magical thinking or the emergence of a saving leader, but through the committed hard work of individual teachers, teams of teachers, groups of students, and communities of concerned adults who are willing to look honestly at the quality of our present experience together, and creatively and collaboratively consider what experiments we can undertake together to make that present more educative for everyone involved.

Central to Dewey's thinking on the present is the belief that teachers, more than members of any profession, must be concerned with taking the "long look ahead." At heart, this means thinking through the long-term ramifications for any habit or idea that is formed in the teacher's classroom. If a student learns that her voice is important and that she can guide her learning into new and ever-expanding interests, this student is on the path to living a more educative future. By contrast, if the student becomes disinterested or disengaged or disempowered, then she is on a mis-, or at least under-, educative path. Here is the way Dewey (2008h) puts it in *Experience and Education*:

I have been forced to speak in general and often abstract language. But what has been said is organically connected with the requirement that experiences in order to be educative must lead out into an expanding world of subject-matter, a subject-matter of facts or information and of ideas. This condition is satisfied only as the educator views teaching and learning as a continuous process of reconstruction of experience. This condition in turn can be satisfied only as the educator has a long look ahead, and views every present experience as a moving force in influencing what future experiences will be. (LW.13.59)

Having the long look ahead means not getting caught up in controversies that generate a lot of sound a fury but do not touch the heart of what it would mean for a student to develop into a more fully educated person. This can be hard, because society seems to want us to get caught up in short-term conflicts, short-term thinking, the tweet that sets off a cable-news cycle that knocks us out of the orbit of meaningful living. But, if we remember that education is about engaging with "an expanding world," I hope we can feel when our vision narrows and when we experience the expansive world of thinking. It is that expansive world that we can hope to dwell in: the world where we are better than we know and where possibilities dwarf fear. And, it is that world we must show our students. While being responsive to the exigencies of our time is important, it is far too easy to get lost in mis-education when we don't have experience with following our thinking and our passion into their expansion and unfolding.

It is for this reason that I find it so important for students to experience what it is like to develop a passion for something, and see what it means to let that passion be surprising enough to change the way we view ourselves, the object of our passion, and how we relate to the object of our passion. To let our feeling of being intrigued by a charter school experiment or the way an author writes about the life of childhood move us to ask the types of questions that upend and unsettle what we thought we knew or believed, not in a way that is destructive, but in a way that opens new lines of thinking that are impossible to not want to go down. Once we have that experience of possibilities quite literally opening to us and inviting our thought, we know what it means to be prepared to engage with the world and our selves in educative ways. The educator needs to learn the art of creating environments and opportunities for students to have these types of experiences. Here is Dewey (2008h) in *Experience and Education* again:

The educator more than the member of any other profession is concerned to have a long look ahead. The physician may feel his job done when he has restored a patient to health. He has undoubtedly the obligation of advising him how to live so as to avoid similar troubles in the future. But, after all, the conduct of his life is his own affair, not the physician's; and what is more important for the present point is that as far as the physician does occupy himself with instruction and advice as to the future of his patient he takes upon himself the function of an educator. The lawyer is occupied with winning a suit for his client or getting the latter out of some complication into which he has got himself. If it goes beyond the case presented to him he too becomes an educator. The educator by the very nature of his work is obliged to see his present work in terms of what it accomplishes, or fails to accomplish, for a future whose objects are linked with those of the present. (LW.13.50)

It is interesting, in the context of this quote, to see that the desire to make the work of teaching more prestigious by linking it—by analogy—to the work of doctors or lawyers neglects the true nature of teaching. While a doctor knows what it means—in most cases—to bring a patient to health, and a lawyer knows when she wins and when she loses, a teacher can never operate with this type of certainty, because her work plays out over the course of a student's lifetime and often travels along indirect channels, and her influence can take a long time to germinate and flower. Saying this, it is important that a teacher not hide behind this fact when a student feels that she is not learning anything in the moment. The claim *I am a teacher, I affect eternity,*[11] *you will understand my teaching later* is clearly not what Dewey is after, even though it is a justification that is not uncommon among educators.

It is important to realize that Dewey is asking an educator to take responsibility for the quality of the educational experience *and* her "present work in terms of what it accomplishes, or fails to accomplish, for a future whose objects are linked with those of the present." This is key. A teacher—through pedagogical exercise and the exercise of pedagogical creativity and judgment—learns to see the impact of her classroom on the formation of habits of mind and heart that live on beyond the immediate moment of instruction. As she sees this impact—say, as she follows the career of her students and hears how they fare after her class—she can begin to adopt ideals and adapt instruction that will allow her students to continuously reconstruct their experiences in educative ways.

This is asking a lot, what may even feel like too much. But, it is exactly why Dewey continually reminds us that we don't have to be seers, we just need to remember what a quality educational experience feels like, and do everything in our power to provide these experiences for students. His focus on the failings of our current way of looking at preparation is not meant to put impossible pressure on us; it is meant to free us of one barrier that gets in the way of providing what we know to be a better educational present for our students. That is, we don't have to worry that we are neglecting our duties as an educator if we don't focus on the old excuse that "you need to learn this because you'll need it later in your education." Instead we can focus on the opportunities involved in seeing a student's broad moral and intellectual growth as our fundamental concern. Here is how Dewey (2008c) puts it—quite beautifully, as I read it—in *School and Society*:

> Why are we so hard of heart and so slow to believe? The imagination is the medium in which the child lives. To him there is everywhere and in everything that occupies his mind and activity at all a surplusage of value and significance. The question of the relation of the school to the child's life is at bottom simply this: Shall we ignore this native setting and tendency, dealing not with the living child at all, but with the dead image we have erected, or shall we give it play and satisfaction? (MW.1.38)

I almost want to let these lines speak for themselves. As a summary of key themes from this book and why they continue to matter, I find this absolutely fitting. Beginning with Dewey's question, I too wonder: Why are we so hard of heart? If you believe, like me, that we are becoming ever more inhumane to children and ever farther away from the promise of American democracy, it may be only natural to respond

with fear and guardedness, but Dewey reminds us that education cannot flourish if we harbor hardened hearts. We must risk vulnerability
and work to create the present we want to see. If we don't see it in our
politics, our pundits, or our policies, we can create it in our classrooms,
in our ways of approaching our students, in the un-hardening of our
hearts and unlocking of fixities that keep us from growth.

When we take this type of risk, we are put back in touch with the
"surplusage of value and significance" that exists in every single child
and in every interaction that we have in our classrooms. Dewey is correct, I believe, to remind us that democracy is enacted and revitalized
not only through critique of injustice and existing institutions, but
also through the unleashing of that surplusage of significance that
exists every moment: right now, in our present. If anything, I hope
this book allows us to appreciate this deep insight on Dewey's part.
His call—to us educators—is to begin cultivating the fullness of each
present moment. As I've tried to stress throughout this book, Dewey
is not calling us to perfection or to judgment: he is inviting us to take
more advantage of the great gifts that always remain close at hand in
any educative relationship.

This way of appreciating Dewey is beautifully summed up by the
final line from the quotation above: "The question of the relation of
the school to the child's life is at bottom simply this: Shall we ignore this
native setting and tendency, dealing not with the living child at all, but
with the dead image we have erected, or shall we give it play and satisfaction?" Shall we continue to live in a dead world, with dead images
that we've erected and have been erected for us, or shall we return to
the living potential of each moment and each child? It is easy to get lost
in waiting and in the very real feeling that we are not where we need to
be and that we seem to be heading in the wrong direction as a society.
But, the school can be a place of life, an engine of reconstruction. Do
we turn to the living potential of each moment and each child, do we
"give it play and satisfaction," or do we fall back on ways of being and
teaching that do not give life?

Play and satisfaction. Teaching is serious work—we are impact-
ing the future—and it is often thankless work. But, Dewey calls us

to re-envision our work as play, the type of play that unsettles what is taken to be natural or fated for us, play that frees a child for her potential and frees us to continuously grow and learn. It is this unsettlement and this freeing for a more educative future that brings deep satisfaction, and that needs to be a greater part of the discourse of teaching and teacher education. Yes, teaching is often underpaid and underappreciated work, but the internal values of continuous growth and being in almost constant touch with the unfurling powers of young people gives a satisfaction and pleasure unlike any other.

We need to remember the satisfactions of learning, and we need to see how helping students get in touch with those satisfactions—right now, in the presents we create with them—may be a better safeguard and promise for a more inclusive and democratic future than any number of more direct attempts at realizing that world. This, at least, is my faith, one derived from Dewey. We need to trust in the transformative power waiting to be found in each educational moment, and find joy and continued growth in the process of creating ways to free that transformative power so that it might remake our world in the image of our best ideals.

# Acknowledgments

I had the good fortune to teach American Philosophies of Education in the spring of 2017, and my wonderful students at St. Lawrence University added a great deal to my appreciation of John Dewey's significance for our time. St. Lawrence University is an ideal place to teach and to be, and I am grateful to the Dean's Office for providing funding that allowed me to purchase access to the collected works of John Dewey.

Working with Purdue University Press has been an excellent experience. The reviewers provided generous and helpful feedback, and this book improved immensely because of their suggestions. They were models of generosity and care, and I cannot thank them enough for their work.

I also want to thank David Hansen. I did not read Dewey before becoming a doctoral student in philosophy and education at Teachers College, and I cannot imagine a better appreciative guide to Dewey than David. His example and continued support are a wonderful presence.

Going back a little further, I don't know if I would've had the confidence or background to become what I am now if it were not for Stanley Bates. Stanley somehow saw something in me that I wasn't sure existed but was trying to will into being, and I will forever be grateful to him and aspire to be the type of professor he was. Stanley's passing in December 2017 was a striking reminder of how much good an educator and an education can do.

As this is a first book, I want to thank my parents. Dedicated educators both, they stand as exemplars of the commitment it takes to live the call to teach.

Lena, Frances, Perry. Though you each are engaged in very different pursuits at the moment I am completing this book—learning to walk, learning to read, learning to be who you are—if any of you ever chance upon this book over the course of your reading, a quick message: I hope your present is as full of love as I feel for each one of you as I write this.

Kiley, I can never thank you enough for giving me back my present, and I look forward with gratitude and hope to all our future presents together.

# Notes

## Preface

1. In particular, this book—using the lens of Dewey's thinking on the present in education—will illuminate aspects of Dewey's educational thinking that remain deeply relevant.

## Introduction

1. This song was first brought to my mind in Wes Anderson's (1998) *Rushmore*. It makes sense now that in an exceptional movie about adolescence and schooling this song would play a role. The line "I am waiting" is repeated over and over in the song, and I feel that this is the soundtrack of the student in too many classrooms.
2. For examples: what role should religion play in school, is it the job of the school to teach values, in the first place, and so on. These explicitly moral questions generate a great deal of dissent, but they may not be the most important questions to ask.
3. For an excellent discussion of this point, see Lampert (1985). For an interesting discussion of discipline for future teachers, see Smith, Fisher, and Frey (2015).
4. The term "hidden curriculum" has taken on an important life of its own after Jackson (1968/1990) coined it. For the sake of my analysis, I am using it in the relatively limited sense Jackson gives it.

5. For another very interesting example, one parallel to Meier's, see Frederick Wiseman's (1968) *High School*, where we very clearly see a connection between authoritarian schooling and an inability to question American politics [a tangential thought: it is interesting to note that this film comes out at the same time as Jackson (1968/1990); it is fascinating to view them as commenting on similar themes central to democracy and education, and equally fascinating that Wiseman chose to document Meier's school experiment in his (1994) *High School II*].

6. The Common Core strikes me as one of the least understood but most ardently discussed educational policies at present. Uniting strange allies across the political spectrum and generating conspiracy theories, we fail to appreciate what the Core is and how it might be used to make the practice of teaching more collaborative and opportunities for learning more ambitious and interesting. I am neither defending nor attacking the Core here, simply stating it as an example of one topic in education that has generated a lot of strong feelings and publicity. And though some of this attention goes where it matters—the qualitative experiences of children in schools—much of it has distracted attention from that. This is my concern. More, there is a large difference between the standards, the ways they are assessed, and the ways these assessments are used to punish teachers and students. One can value the standards while objecting to the ways they are assessed: This often gets lost in the noise of debates on the standards.

7. In my reading, I have not found writing in education that treats John Dewey's thinking on the educational present in a direct and sustained way, though Granger (2006) offers an insightful discussion at points in his narrative. The closest I found is Stroud's (2011) work on moral cultivation and the aesthetics of living in the present. This work informs my reading of Dewey, though I don't see the work as close enough to what I am doing to necessitate a full scholarly discussion of Stroud. Kestenbaum (2002), Pappas (2008), and Rockefeller (1991) have interesting insight into John Dewey's thinking on the present as well, but—again—not enough to merit a full scholarly discussion before embarking on my own project here.

8. For notable examples, see Dewey (2008a–i).

9. Note, the present doesn't *prepare* us for the future. As Dewey clearly shows, the only way to bring about a future worthy of our ideals is living a present imbued with those ideals. That work can—and needs to—start now.

10. This echo from Dewey's (2008h) *Experience and Education* is beautifully expanded upon in Jackson (2011).

## Chapter 1

1. For citations of Dewey I will use a bit of a hybrid system. I will use more of a formal APA style with the dates so readers can easily find the reference in the works cited. I will also use the standard practice of LW.13.5 when giving the page number. In the case that the reader is not familiar with this practice, the LW refers to Dewey's later works (EW is early works and MW is middle words), the next number (13) refers to the volume of the later works the citation is found in, and the final number (5) refers to the page number.

2. As a quick Google search will demonstrate, there are Americans who feel that Dewey is responsible for just about every ill that has befallen public education in America. And, a more scholarly approach does not always cast him in a more favorable light. Just recently Frank Margonis (2009) has argued that Dewey's approach to education was only intended for European American students; as such, adhering to his philosophy will marginalize and mis-educate African American students. For an overview of this issue, see Frank (2013a).

3. A striking example of this is Stanley Cavell's uncharacteristically uncareful reading of Dewey. Cavell is one of the most interesting and exciting thinkers I know, especially when he engages with his favorite interlocutors like Emerson and Wittgenstein (for examples, Cavell [1990; 1999]). His engagement with Dewey is far too often with the lesser, rather than the greater Dewey. For an excellent discussion of this point, see Jackson (1992).

4. For example, Hansen's (2006) edited volume on *Democracy and Education* and Furman's (2015) work on inclusive education. Again, there are far too many to enumerate.

5. I see a wonderful example of working from practice and into philosophy in the wonderful work of Sherman (2013). Hers too is an example of the reconstructed dualism Dewey warned of.

6. This is, of course, a very cursory discussion, which feels permissible given that this is not a major focus of my study. For examples of excellent work on the topic, see Jackson (2012), Johnson (2006), Higgins (2008), and Stengel (2001).

7. Dewey's quietism has not been a focus in the literature on Dewey, likely because—as mentioned above—scholarly attention has not focused on Dewey's thinking on the present. For an interesting discussion of contemporary quietist thinking, see Perl, Griffiths, Evans, and Davis (2009) and the fascinating symposiums that run in the issues of *Common Knowledge* following this introduction. For a classic in the tradition, see De Caussade (1741/1982).

8. Dewey (2008a) has a beautiful description of this as it relates to college in EW.3.54–55.

9. For a discussion of Dewey and love, see Garrison (1997).

10. For a beautiful discussion of mindfulness and education, see Hill (2006).

11. Tolstoy considered the *Calendar of Wisdom* his greatest gift to mankind, and this work—like his *Gospel in Brief* (Tolstoy, 1883/1997a)—is focused on living in the present. A close reader of this work, Ludwig Wittgenstein (1921/1999) remarks in his *Tractatus* that "eternal life belongs to those who live in the present" (p. 72).

12. There is a lot of literature on white privilege or privilege in education. For one discussion, see Frank (2013b). For a criticism of Tolstoy from the perspective of privilege, see de Beauvoir (1949/2011).

13. Bruner's (1960) idea of the "spiral curriculum" is a good example of what this might look like. As well, the more we learn about learning, the more we see just how prescient and important Dewey's thinking on the present as it relates to learning is (Bransford, Brown, and Cocking, 1999). As well, Bard College's early high schools are excellent examples of how students can do meaningful work in the present; they don't have to wait until college to start thinking.

14. This concern/criticism is very much alive. There is a real concern that we are preparing students for the early 20th century when the world that they will live and work in will be very different from that world.

15. For an interesting sociological discussion of this phenomenon, see Hochschild (2016).

16. For a very Deweyan discussion of reverence, see Rud and Garrison (2010).

17. Again, a quick Google search can show the vitriol spewed at Dewey, someone who both espoused and wrote in the most mannerly way and who is completely undeserving of this type of treatment.

18. It is far easier to criticize the lesser Dewey than try to understand his positive project. Edmundson (2006) is a classic example of pseudo-scholarship in this vein. A decent critique of lesser Dewey, possibly, but it is very clear that Dewey is not an acolyte of Rousseau, though lesser readers of Dewey pin him to Rousseau to then paint Dewey as an ideological proponent of progressive practices of which he is highly critical.

19. I think this point is nicely made—in a more conservative vein—by MacIntyre (1981).

20. This, again, shows why Dewey's thinking on the present cannot be adequately captured by the instrumentalist or the quietist.

21. The line is also from Emerson's (1844/1983b) essay "Experience." For an illuminating discussion of paltry empiricism, see Granger (2003).

22. For a discussion of this, see Frank (2017).

23. Work like Bransford, Brown, and Cocking (2000) and Glaser, Chudowsky, and Pelligrino (2001).

24. For a nice discussion of this, see Diamond (1991).

25. All of Paley's work is worth reading. For a good start, see Paley (2005). For a good discussion of a Deweyan approach to letting experience revise our theories, see E. Anderson (1998).

26. For an excellent discussion of Danish forest schools, see Wagner (2004). For a compelling video—which is a student favorite in my college classroom—Google "Kids Gone Wild: Denmark's Forest Kindergartens." I had the great good fortune to spend time in Danish schools, and it was remarkable watching my seven-year-old daughter Lena absolutely blossom in a matter of minutes in the new and wonderful learning environment that was Ravenholm. I thank my colleague Erin McCarthy for inviting me to teach with her in Denmark, all of the students who traveled and learned with us, Maja Sbahi Biehl at DIS for setting up our summer semester, and all of the wonderful people—students, teachers, administrators—who opened their schools to us over the course of the summer.

27. For a very nice discussion of Deweyan childhood, see Burdick-Shepherd (2013). As well, see Diamond (2008).

28. For a very good discussion of pragmatic hope, within the context of urban education but transferrable across educational contexts, see Noguera (2003).

29. It is interesting to consider how many modernist novels are somehow centered around a dystopian vision of school, where school becomes the site of repression if not outright torture; for two excellent examples, see: Walser (1909/1999) and Gombrowicz (1937/2012). I also see this at work in James Joyce; for a nice discussion, see Kiberd (2010).

## Chapter 2

1. It is important to revisit *Experience and Education* because as Dewey's last attempt to formulate his thinking on education in a clear and direct manner, I think it must be seen as a key source in any attempt to understand Dewey's approach to education. More, and as mentioned in chapter 1, Dewey—through this work—sought to distance himself from the forms of education his thinking inspired.

2. As mentioned in chapter 1, "progressive" is used here as shorthand—as Dewey uses it in *Experience and Education*—for the family of "new" approaches to education his philosophical work inspired.

3. For example, we see that in many KIPP schools there is a complete focus on helping students meet goals and so that they can attend selective colleges that would've likely been otherwise out of reach (for a balanced and recent discussion of charters, see Kahlenberg and Potter, 2014). And, as Lisa Delpit (1995; 2013) argues, progressive education done poorly often fails to meet the needs of students who need it most. So, while there are positives to traditional approaches to education, and while they may indeed be better than many progressive approaches that are overly permissive and undereducative, they are not—as I hope to show—to be preferred to the type of education Dewey champions.

4. For example, Bard High School Early College is a program that believes young people can begin doing serious college-level work in high school.

It is the waiting to do the serious work that often turns students away from learning; a no-excuses approach only exacerbates this.

5. It is hard to enumerate all the ways that the social-education system falls away from our ideals. For just one excellent example of this, see Berliner (2006). As anyone familiar with educational research knows, there is a great deal of work on systemic injustice and inequality in education.

6. For excellent discussions of how we can do this type of work with children see Levy (1996) and Berger (2003).

7. Here we can return to the work of Debbie Meier referenced in the introduction. Her students needed to *demonstrate* habits of mind that were valuable in order to graduate; they did real work in school; school wasn't a mere preparation to do real work after graduation. And, these students were still able to get into college and do well once they got there. For research on the effectiveness of Meier's work, see Duckor and Perlstein (2014).

8. One of the most beautiful and powerful examples of this is Bard College's work in prison. This work stands as a testament—like their work in high schools—to the transformative power of the liberal arts. For a good discussion, see Lagemann (2011).

9. Discussed above in chapter 1.

10. For a more generous—and frankly accurate—reading of Dewey's thinking in *A Common Faith* see Hickman (2016). As Dewey makes very clear in this work, one can appreciate the religious spirit that animates religions without believing in the doctrines of any organized church.

11. Although things like differentiated instruction are criticized for being activity for activities sake, this cannot be further from the truth, because differentiated instruction is driven by ambitious learning goals (Tomlinson, 2001). Understanding by Design is an approach to curriculum design that is adamant that a learning experience must be engaging *and* educative, and it offers a clear path toward realizing this type of curriculum (Wiggins & McTighe, 2005).

12. I see something similar going on in the un-schooling movement. While there are many ways in which formal schooling can be mis-educative, simply getting rid of the structure of school and allowing children to "choose" what they learn may often turn out to be more mis-educative

(though, like all things, some approaches to un-schooling may be quite educative).

13. For an excellent overview and discussion, see Stitzlein (2017).

14. There are many useful critiques of this type of multicultural education. For one prominent and useful text, see Nieto (2009).

15. For a discussion of knowingness, see Frank (2015).

16. As mentioned above, this is a point made over and again by Wiggins and McTighe (2005).

17. Hence the importance of pedagogical judgment/manner (Fenstermacher, 2001) or tact (Manen, 1991).

18. It is for this reason that approximations of practice and performance-based assessments are so important. For more on these, see Windschitl, Thompson, and Braaten (2011) and Dede (2013).

19. Note, that I am critical of watered-down versions of these approaches. When done well, differentiated instruction grounded in constructivist learning theory is highly effective, even if it is challenging—but by no means impossible—to realize (Lawrence-Brown, 2004; Subban, 2006; Airasian & Walsh, 1997).

20. For example, one need only be in the classroom with a nationally board-certified teacher or other "master teacher" to get a palpable sense for this type of engaged learning.

21. For a good description of schools that do this type of work, see Martinez and McGrath (2014) and Ritchart (2015).

22. For a trenchant and direct criticism of "at risk" rhetoric—along with many other topics—see Berliner and Glass (2014). For looks at the game of school, see Pope (2003) and Fried (2005).

23. Much has been written about the importance of transfer in learning. For some examples, see: Wittrock (1974), Haskell (2000), Bransford, Brown, and Cocking (2000), and Wiggins and McTighe (2005).

24. To watch the video, visit: https://www.youtube.com/watch?v=K Zomm-1BbYQ

25. For two very nice practical discussions of the affective dimensions of learning, see Wormeli (2003) and Tovani (2011).

26. It has taken me a while to appreciate this aspect of Dewey's thought. Dewey respects us enough to want to make his point in measured prose;

he is not attempting to sway us with rhetoric that makes us followers of thinkers and not advocates of thought. At the same time, the passion is there: Dewey is an impassioned advocate of education, and this shines through with careful attention to his prose.

27. Much more can be said on this point. It is the heart of Dewey's thinking in *Democracy and Education*. For an excellent collection on this work, see Hansen (2006).

28. Here I am thinking of Barthes (1975).

29. For a very interesting line of thought with a lot of similarities between the position I am advancing here, see Rodgers and Raider-Roth's (2006) thinking on *presence* in teaching. As well, I find significant and interesting overlap between this position and Setiya's (2014) fascinating thinking on midlife.

30. I find it interesting that right around the point in the *Tractatus* when Wittgenstein (1921/1999) writes about living in the present he also writes about how the world of a happy man is quite literally *different* from the world of the unhappy.

31. For an interesting discussion of this phenomenon, see Kierkegaard (1847/2009), especially part I, chapter 1.

32. Here I think of Michael Oakeshott's (2001) wonderful discussion of *style* in teaching.

33. I completely agree with Doris Santoro's (2011a) deeply insightful analysis that policies surrounding teaching have caused many teachers to feel demoralized, so I want to avoid that.

34. This, in many ways, is Robert Frost's approach to poetry education. I wrote my dissertation on Frost as an educator and philosopher of education, and a brief synopsis can be found in Frank (2007).

35. Wiggins and McTighe (2005) offer an excellent discussion of the differences between covering and uncovering.

36. For a beautiful and moving discussion of attention, see Weil (1970).

## Chapter 3

1. Here I am echoing the distinction William James (1907/1998) makes. As James shows in *Pragmatism*, it is often those who claim to be the most tough-minded who avoid the hard work of realizing ideals.

2. For a nice recent discussion of how to do this type of teaching, see Burns and Botzakis (2016).

3. Hope in this direction may be foolhardy. As I write, Betsy DeVos is our Secretary of Education. Instead of learning from our educational experiments, I fear that ideology may trump evidence, leading us further away from the ideal of educating every student as effectively as we know how.

4. This is why I love that Darling-Hammond and Sykes (1999) refer to teaching as the learning profession. Teachers never simply implement or deliver curriculum; as they grow and learn, they become more educatively present and represent the curriculum. See also Feiman-Nemser (2012).

5. In some ways, it might be helpful to see some parallels with the thinking of Immanuel Kant here. So long as we accept our moral aims from the outside, we don't act ethically. In order to act ethically, we need to have reverence for the fact that we can give ourselves our own law and then work to realize it in the world. For some excellent contemporary discussions of Kant see Herman (2008), Korsgaard (1996), and O'Neill (2014).

6. For a beautiful discussion of the significance of turning or conversation in our ethical life, see Cavell (1999).

7. I use responsive deliberately. Culturally responsive pedagogy is extraordinarily important, and the insights of culturally responsive educators are useful to every teacher regardless of the composition of their classroom. There is a lot of literature on the topic, but a great place to start and return to as we think about this topic is Villegas and Lucas (2002).

8. Though I can't go into this in any depth here, I think the *expressive* dimensions of what we do as teachers deserves far more attention than they are often given. For more on the expressive in ethics, see Anderson (1995).

9. For a good discussion of how to facilitate this in teacher education, see Sockett (2012).

10. For an excellent discussion of moralism and its attendant dangers, see Diamond (1997).

11. The idea of channeling energy strikes me as a very important one, and one that has been the focus on many American pragmatist writers. For two very interesting discussions, see Poirier (1987, 1992).

12. For a beautiful discussion of this type of learning, see Duckworth (2006).

13. For an interesting—if controversial—discussion of this ironic stance, see Wampole (2012).

14. For an excellent discussion of the game of school that is still—sadly—relevant, see Powell, Farrar, and Cohen (1985).

15. For more on this, see the essay "I, Thou, and It," in Hawkins (1974).

16. For an excellent discussion of finding this balance, see Daniels and Zemelman (2014).

17. For a beautiful discussion of this, see Poirier (1987).

18. For an extraordinarily powerful demonstration of this, see Alexander (2010). For a discussion of Dewey's potential limitations regarding his own understanding of racism as an impediment to growth, see Frank (2013a).

19. As discussed throughout this book, education is not toward some fixed end—vocational education for trades, academic education for college—instead it is about responding to the needs of the present moment that one claims an education.

20. For a nice discussion of this, with specific relation to the work of John Stuart Mill—someone Dewey admired—see Anderson (1991).

21. For a good discussion of Emerson and transitions, see Levin (1999).

22. For a good discussion of the concept of "what works" in education, see Biesta (2010).

## Chapter 4

1. For a very interesting and important discussion of how one creates a meaningful life, see Wolf (2012).

2. Fear is often *the* stumbling block in education. For more on this topic, see Shklar (1989) and Nussbaum (2012).

3. It is interesting just how central the concept of *experience* is to Dewey's work, notably, in this context, *Experience and Education.* For an engaging discussion of Dewey on experience, see Hohr (2013).

4. See the section "Childhood as Golden Impossibility" in chapter 1 of this book for a discussion of what I mean by using the term impossible here.

5. The language of avoidance and acknowledgment is meant to call to mind the extraordinarily important work of Stanley Cavell (1999). For a great look at Cavell's significance for education, see Saito and Standish (2012).

6. For a beautiful discussion of responsiveness, see Sherman (2013).

7. I found it fascinating, while reading Green's (2014) deeply engaging book

on teacher education, that the new approach to teaching and teacher education Deborah Ball was developing and had difficulty labeling she simply called *that type of teaching.*

8. It may go without saying, but it is important to note that students seem to be able to tell the difference between the teacher who genuinely cares and who is trying to care because she thinks she should.

9. For more on this narrative, see Goldstein's (2014) wonderful book on teaching.

10. Note that I don't use the word experience. For a wonderful discussion of how fraught experience is in teacher preparation, see Feiman-Nemser and Buchmann (1985).

11. For a detailed and moving description of these internal rewards, see Sherman (2013).

12. Here, I am reminded of James (1899/1992) reminding students that to miss the adventure in another person's experience is to miss everything. For a brief discussion of missing the adventure, see Diamond (1985); for a longer discussion, see Diamond (1997).

13. For a wonderful, philosophically rich discussion of democracy and habits, see Hansen and James (2016). Though I don't engage the literature devoted to Dewey's thinking on habit, one might consult Shusterman (2012) for a discussion of embodiment and habit, and Schoenbach (2012) for a beautiful discussion of pragmatism, modernism, and habit. As mentioned earlier in the book, my goal is not to engage the literature on Dewey directly; rather, my aim is to help us think with Dewey.

14. For a bit more of a direct indictment that seems to overstate what is a very real problem, see Deresiewicz (2014).

15. For a recent look at how well high school students are prepared for college, see Butrymowicz (2017).

16. For an excellent discussion of the role of "experience" in teacher education, see Feiman-Nemser and Buchmann (1985). This relates to Lortie's (1975) thinking on the apprenticeship of observation. For further discussion of this phenomenon, see Grossman (1991).

17. For a very insightful and interesting discussion of spirituality and teaching, see Lichtmann (2005).

18. Taken from Auden's (1989) early untitled poem beginning "Sir, no man's enemy . . ." (p. 7).

## Conclusion

1. In this time, one of the voices I find most realistic and reassuring is that of Canadian philosopher Charles Taylor. For a good example of his thinking, see http://www.cbc.ca/radio/thesunday edition/the-trudeau-vacation-saying-no-to-chemo-marjorie-harris -retires-charles-taylor-on-trump-1.3941092/charles-taylor-s-clear-eyed -vision-of-our-distress-coupled-to-a-deep-rooted-celebration-of-humanity -1.3941096

2. I expect readers may be familiar with this. In case they are not, here is a good place to start for an overview: http://www.middlebury.edu/newsroom /information-on-charles-murray-visit

3. I say understandably confused given that our President has no experience as an elected official and given the fact that the veracity of many of his statements—from the size of his inaugural crowd to the claim that President Obama tapped his phones—are indeed hard to substantiate. Note, I am trying to not make an evaluative judgment here (though one could be made), just a descriptive one.

4. Middlebury is quick to note that a student group invited this speaker, but it is also the case that the event was co-sponsored by an academic department at the College. The line between allowing a group to invite a speaker and the College endorsing the speaker may be clear after the fact and to administrators, but I imagine it may not have looked or felt that way to students.

5. Most notably, the Southern Poverty Law Center.

6. In this way, my position is very much aligned with that of William James (1908/1988). The liberal arts graduate should—at the very least—know how to recognize excellence, in all its forms, and the liberal arts environment is one where students are immersed in a world of excellence that fortifies, provokes and inspires them to support, advocate for, create, and live excellence.

7. Free speech and the free exchange of ideas—even wrongheaded, reprehensible ideas—is deeply important. We can admit that, and still wonder about the specifically educational value of college-endorsed or college-allowed speakers who spout wrongheaded or reprehensive ideas. As I was

completing this volume, Ben-Porath (2017) published a wonderful take on these issues. I cannot fully engage with her argument here, though I heartily recommend it.

8.  As I finalize this book, students are protesting gun violence. Protests like this will likely continue into the future, and we can stand outside and either praise or blame these students, or we can engage—in a spirit of learning and education—with these students so that their desire for justice can be channeled to better, not worse, outcomes.

9.  In response to student unrest in the 60s, Wolin and Schaar (1970) thought deeply about the democratic and educationally possibilities of student protests. I look forward to work like this emerging from, and for, our own time.

10. Even though it goes without saying, I want to make clear my deep gratefulness to Middlebury and my deep hope for my students at St. Lawrence University. Far from feeling like I was being anything like "indoctrinated into liberal ways," I felt so deeply respected, cared for, and challenged at Middlebury that it caused me to want to share the life-changing power of education with my own students, hoping—knowing the odds—that I might end up where I am today. I must single out Stanley Bates and Dan Brayton for showing how relationships formed between a teacher and student can give students confidence and direction they would've never known possible if not for the relationship with a teacher. All this loose and demeaning talk about ideological bias in higher education often renders us incapable of remembering or appreciating the life-giving power of teaching and learning that happens at places like Middlebury, St. Lawrence, and other small liberal arts colleges.

11. To use the oft quoted but often decontextualized line from Henry Adams (1903/1983).

# References

Adams, H. (1983). *The education of Henry Adams*. New York: Library of America. (Original work published 1903)

Airasian, P. W., & Walsh, M. E. (1997). Constructivist cautions. *Phi Delta Kappan, 78*(6), 444–449.

Alexander, M. (2010). *The new Jim Crow*. New York: New Press.

Anderson, E. (1991). John Stuart Mill and experiments in living. *Ethics, 102*(1), 4–26.

Anderson, E. (1995). *Value in ethics and economics*. Cambridge, MA: Harvard University Press.

Anderson, E. (1998). Pragmatism, science and moral inquiry. In R. Fox & R. Westbrook (Eds.), *In the face of facts* (pp. 10–39). New York: Cambridge University Press.

Anderson, E. (2010). *The imperative of integration*. Princeton, NJ: Princeton University Press.

Anderson, W. (1998). *Rushmore* [Motion picture]. United States of America: Criterion.

Auden, W. H. (1989). *Selected poems*. New York: Vintage.

Barthes, R. (1975). *The pleasure of the text*. (R. Miller, Trans.). New York: Hill and Wang.

Baurain, B. (2011). Common ground with *A Common Faith*: Dewey's idea of the "religious." *Education and Culture, 27*(2), 74–91.

Ben-Porath, S. (2017). *Free speech on campus*. Philadelphia: University of Pennsylvania Press.

Berger, R. (2003). *An ethic of excellence*. Portsmouth, NH: Heinemann.

Berliner, D. (2006). Our impoverished view of educational research. *Teachers College Record, 108*(6), 949–995.

Berliner, D., & Glass, G. (2014). *50 myths and lies that threaten America's public schools*. New York: Teachers College Press.

Berry, W. (2015). *Our only world*. Berkeley, CA: Counterpoint.

Biesta, J. J. (2010). Why 'what works' still won't work: From evidence-based education to value-based education. *Studies in Philosophy and Education, 29*(5), 491–503.

Bransford, J. D., Brown, A. L., & Cocking, R. R. (2000). *How people learn* [Expanded edition]. Washington, DC: National Academies Press.

Bruner, J. (1960). *The process of education*. Cambridge, MA: Harvard University Press.

Burdick-Shepherd, S. (2013). Rediscovering morality through the concept of childhood. *Yearbook of the National Society for the Study of Education, 112*(1), 98–115.

Burns, L. D., & Botzakis, S. (2016). *Teach on purpose*. New York: Teachers College Press.

Butrymowicz, S. (2017). Most colleges enroll many students who aren't prepared for higher education. *The Hechinger Report*. Retrieved from http://hechingerreport.org/colleges-enroll-students-arent-prepared-higher-education/

Cavell, S. (1990). *Conditions handsome and unhandsome*. Chicago: University of Chicago Press.

Cavell, S. (1999). *The claim of reason*. New York: Oxford.

Csikszentmihalyi, M. (1990). *Flow: The psychology of optimal experience*. New York: Harper.

Daniels, H., & Zemelman, S. (2014). *Subjects matter* (2nd ed.). Portsmouth, NH: Heinemann.

Darling-Hammond, L., & Sykes, G. (1999). *Teaching as the learning profession*. San Francisco, CA: Jossey-Bass.

Davidow, W. H., & Malone, M. S. (2014). What happens to society when robots replace workers? *Harvard Business Review*. Retrieved from https://hbr.org/2014/12/what-happens-to-society-when-robots-replace-workers

de Beauvoir, S. (2011). *The second sex*. (C. Borde & S. Malovany-Chevallier, Trans.). New York: Vintage. (Original work published 1949)

De Cayssade, J. P. (1982). *The sacrament of the present moment.* (K. Muggeridge, Trans.). New York: Harper Collins. (Original work published 1741)

Dede, C. (2013). Opportunities and challenges in embedding diagnostic assessments into immersive interfaces. *Educational Designer, 2*(6), 1–22.

Delpit, L. (1995). *Other people's children.* New York: New Press.

Delpit, L. (2013). *"Multiplication is for white people": Raising expectations for other people's children.* New York: New Press.

Deresiewicz, W. (2014). *Excellent sheep.* New York: Free Press.

Dewey, E., & Dewey, J. (2008). *Schools of to-morrow.* In J. A. Boydston (Ed.), *John Dewey: The middle works, 1899–1924* (Vol. 8). Carbondale: Southern Illinois University Press.

Dewey, J. (2008a). College course: What should I expect from it? In J. A. Boydston (Ed.), *John Dewey: The early works, 1882–1898* (Vol. 3, pp. 51–55). Carbondale: Southern Illinois University Press.

Dewey, J. (2008b). Self-realization as moral ideal. In J. A. Boydston (Ed.), *John Dewey: The early works, 1882–1898* (Vol. 4, pp. 42–53). Carbondale: Southern Illinois University Press.

Dewey, J. (2008c). *School and society.* In J. A. Boydston (Ed.), *John Dewey: The middle works, 1899–1924* (Vol. 1). Carbondale: Southern Illinois University Press.

Dewey, J. (2008d). *Moral principles in education.* In J. A. Boydston (Ed.), *John Dewey: The middle works, 1899–1924* (Vol. 4). Carbondale: Southern Illinois University Press.

Dewey, J. (2008e). *Democracy and education.* In J. A. Boydston (Ed.), *John Dewey: The middle works, 1899–1924* (Vol. 9). Carbondale: Southern Illinois University Press.

Dewey, J. (2008f). *Sources of a science of education.* In J. A. Boydston (Ed.), *John Dewey: The later works, 1925–1953* (Vol. 5). Carbondale: Southern Illinois University Press.

Dewey, J. (2008g). Self-saver or Frankenstein? [Book review]. In J. A. Boydston (Ed.), *John Dewey: The later works, 1925–1953* (Vol. 6, pp. 280–285). Carbondale: Southern Illinois University Press.

Dewey, J. (2008h). *Experience and education.* In J. A. Boydston (Ed.), *John Dewey: The later works, 1925–1953* (Vol. 13). Carbondale: Southern Illinois University Press.

Dewey, J. (2008i). Between two worlds. In J. A. Boydston (Ed.), *John Dewey: The later works, 1925–1953* (Vol. 17, pp. 451–465). Carbondale: Southern Illinois University Press.

Diamond, C. (1985). Missing the adventure. *Journal of Philosophy, 82*(10), 530–531.

Diamond, C. (1991). Knowing tornadoes and other things. *New Literary History, 22*(4), 1001–1015.

Diamond, C. (1997). Henry James, moral philosophers, moralism. *The Henry James Review, 18*(3), 243–257.

Diamond, J. (2008). *Welcome to the aquarium.* New York: New Press.

Dixit, J. (2008). The art of now: Six steps to living in the moment. *Psychology Today.* Retrieved from https://www.psychologytoday.com/articles/200811/the-art-now-six-steps-living-in-the-moment

Duckor, B., & Perlstein, D. (2014). Assessing habits of mind: Teaching to the test at Central Park East Secondary School. *Teachers College Record, 116*(2), 1–33.

Duckworth, E. (2006). *The having of wonderful ideas.* New York: Teachers College Press.

Dweck, C. (2006). *Mindset.* New York: Penguin.

Edmundson, H. T. (2006). *John Dewey and the decline of American education.* Wilmington, DE: ISI Books.

Emerson, R. W. (1983a). "Self-Reliance," in *Essays and lectures.* New York: Library of America. (Original work published 1841)

Emerson, R. W. (1983b). "Experience," in *Essays and lectures.* New York: Library of America. (Original work published 1844)

Feiman-Nemser, S. (2012). *Teachers as learners.* Cambridge, MA: Harvard Education Press.

Feiman-Nemser, S., & Buchmann, M. (1985). Pitfalls of experience in teacher preparation. *Teachers College Record, 87*(1), 53–65.

Fenstermacher, G. D. (2001). On the concept of manner and its visibility in teaching practice. *Journal of Curriculum Studies, 33*(6), 639–653.

Forzani, F. M. (2014). Understanding "core practices" and "practice-based" teacher education: Learning from the past. *Journal of Teacher Education, 65*(4), 357–368.

Fox, R. W., & Westbrook, R. B. (1998). *In the face of facts.* New York: Cambridge University Press.

Frank, J. (2007). The notebooks of Robert Frost. *Teachers College Record.* Retrieved from https://www.tcrecord.org/content.asp?contentid=13835

Frank, J. (2013a). Reconstructing Deweyan growth: The significance of James Baldwin's moral psychology. *Education and Culture, 29*(2), 121–132.

Frank, J. (2013b). Mitigating against epistemic injustice in educational research. *Educational Researcher, 42*(7), 363–370.

Frank, J. (2015). Love and growth: On one aspect of James Baldwin's significance for education. *Teachers College Record, 117*(9), 1–38.

Frank, J. (2017). Realizing a democratic community of teachers: John Dewey and the idea of a science of education. *Education Sciences, 7,* 1–10.

Fried, R. (2005). *The game of school.* San Francisco, CA: Jossey-Bass.

Furman, C. (2015). "Why I am not a painter": Developing an inclusive classroom. *Education and Culture, 31*(1), 61–76.

Garrison, J. (1997). *Dewey and eros.* New York: Teachers College Press.

Gay, G. (2010). *Culturally responsive teaching.* New York: Teachers College Press.

Gilliam, W. S., Maupin, A. N., Reyes, C. R., Accavitti, M. & Shic, F. (2016). Do early educators' implicit biases regarding sex and race relate to behavior expectations and recommendations of preschool expulsions and suspensions? Yale University Child Study Center. Retrieved from https://medicine.yale.edu/childstudy/zigler/publications/Preschool%20Implicit%20Bias%20Policy%20Brief_final_9_26_276766_5379_v1.pdf

Glaser, R., Chudowsky, N., & Pelligrino, J. W. (2001). *Knowing what they know.* Washington, DC: National Academies Press.

Goldstein, D. (2014). *The teacher wars.* New York: Doubleday.

Gombrowicz (2012). *Ferdydurke* (D. Borchardt, Trans.). New Haven, CT: Yale University Press. (Original work published 1937)

Gordon, M. (2007). Living the questions: Rilke's challenge to our quest for certainty. *Educational Theory, 57*(1), 37–52.

Granger, D. (2003). Positivism, skepticism, and the attractions of "paltry empiricism": Stanley Cavell and the current standards movement in education. *Philosophy of Education Yearbook, 2003,* 146–154.

Granger, D. (2006). *John Dewey, Robert Pirsig, and the art of living.* New York: Palgrave.

Green, E. (2014). *Building a better teacher.* New York: Norton.

Grossman, P. (1991). Overcoming the apprenticeship of observation in teacher education coursework. *Teaching and Teacher Education, 7*(4), 345–357.

Grossman, P., McDonald, M., Hammermas, K., & Ronfeldt, M. (2008). Dismantling dichotomies in teacher education. In M. Cochran-Smith, S. Feiman-Nemster, D. J. McIntyre, & K. E. Demers (Eds.), *Handbook of research on teacher education: Enduring questions in changing contexts* (243–248). New York: Routledge.

Hadot, P. (1995). *Philosophy as a way of life.* (M. Chase, Trans.). New York: Blackwell.

Hansen, D. T. (2001). *Exploring the moral heart of teaching: Toward a teacher's creed.* New York: Teachers College Press.

Hansen, D. T. (2004). A poetics of teaching. *Educational Theory, 54*(2), 119–142.

Hansen, D. T. (2006). *John Dewey and our educational prospect.* Albany, NY: SUNY Press.

Hansen, D.T. (2018). Bearing witness to the fusion of person and role in teaching. *The Journal of Aesthetic Education, 52*(4), 21–48.

Hansen, D. T., & James, C. (2016). The importance of cultivating democratic habits in schools. *Journal of Curriculum Studies, 48*(1), 94–112.

Haskell, R. E. (2000). *Transfer of learning.* New York: Academic Press.

Hawkins, D. (1974). *The informed vision.* New York: Agathan.

Hawkins, D. (2000). *The roots of literacy.* Boulder, CO: University Press of Colorado.

Hearne, V. (1986). *Adam's task.* New York: Knopf.

Herman, B. (2008). *Moral literacy.* Cambridge, MA: Harvard University Press.

Hewitt, B. (2014). *Home grown.* Boston: Roost.

Hickman, L. (2016). What we can teach when we teach (about) religion. *Education and Culture, 32*(2), 4–17.

Higgins, C. (2008). Instrumentalism and the clichés of aesthetic education: A Deweyan corrective. *Education and Culture, 24*(1), 6–19.

Hill, C. (2006). Introduction: Contemplative practice and education. *Teachers College Record, 108*(9), 1723–1732.

Hochschild, A. R. (2016). *Strangers in their own land.* New York: New Press.

Hohr, H. (2013). The concept of experience by John Dewey revisted. *Studies in Philosophy and Education, 32*(1), 25–38.

Hopkins, G. M. (1877). God's grandeur. Retrieved from https://www.poetryfoundation.org/poems-and-poets/poems/detail/44395

Hughes, L. (1951). Harlem. Retrieved from https://www.poetryfoundation.org/poems/46548/harlem

Jackson, P. W. (1990). *Life in classrooms*. New York: Teachers College Press. (Original work published 1968)

Jackson, P. W. (1992). *Untaught lessons*. New York: Teachers College Press.

Jackson, P. W. (2002). Dewey's 1906 definition of art. *Teachers College Record*, *104*(2), 167–177.

Jackson, P. W. (2011). *What is education*. Chicago: University of Chicago Press.

Jackson, P. W. (2012). How we think we think. *Teachers College Record*, *114*(2), 1–17.

Jackson, P. W., Boostrom, R. E., & Hansen, D. T. (1998). *The moral life of schools*. San Francisco, CA: Jossey-Bass.

James, W. (1988). The Social Value of the College-Bred, in *William James: Writings 1902–1910*. New York: Library of America. (Original work published 1908)

James, W. (1992). *Talks to teachers* in *William James: Writings 1878–1899*. New York: Library of America. (Original work published 1899)

James, W. (1998). *Pragmatism*. Cambridge, MA: Harvard University Press. (Original work published 1907)

Jennings, P. (2015). *Mindfulness for teachers*. New York: Norton.

Johnson, J. S. (2006). *Inquiry and education*. Albany: SUNY Press.

Kahlenberg, R. D., & Potter, H. (2014). *A smarter charter*. New York: Teachers College Press.

Kennedy, M. M. (1999). The role of preservice teacher education. In L. Darling-Hammond & G. Sykes (Eds.), *Teaching as the learning profession: Handbook of teaching and policy* (pp. 54–86). San Francisco, CA: Jossey-Bass.

Kennedy, M. M. (2016). Parsing the practice of teaching. *Journal of Teacher Education*, *67*(1), 6–17.

Kestenbaum, V. (2002). *The grace and severity of the ideal*. Chicago: University of Chicago Press.

Kiberd, D. (2010). Ulysses *and us: The art of the everyday life in Joyce's masterpiece*. New York: Norton.

Kierkegaard, S. (2009). *Works of love*. (H. & E. Hong, Trans.). New York: Harper. (Original work published 1847)

Kirp, D. (2015). *Improbable scholars*. New York: Oxford University Press.

Korsgaard, C. (1996). *Creating the kingdom of ends*. New York: Cambridge University Press.

Labaree, D. F. (2012). *Someone has to fail*. Cambridge, MA: Harvard University Press.

Lagemann, E. C. (2011). What can college mean? Lessons from the Bard Prison Initiative. *Change: The Magazine of Higher Learning, 43*(6), 14–19.

Lampert, M. (1985). How do teachers manage to teach? *Harvard Education Review, 55*(2), 178–195.

Lawrence-Brown, D. (2004). Differentiated instruction: Inclusive strategies for standards-based learning that benefit the whole class. *American Secondary Education, 32*(3), 34–63.

Lee, H.-S., & Butler, L. (2003). Making authentic science accessible to students. *International Journal of Science Education, 25*(8), 923–948.

Levin, J. (1999). *The poetics of transition.* Durham, NC: Duke University Press.

Levy, S. (1996). *Starting from scratch.* Portsmouth, NH: Heinemann.

Lewis, C., & Hurd, J. (2011). *Lesson study step by step.* Portsmouth, NH: Heinemann.

Lichtmann, M. (2005). *The teacher's way: Teaching and contemplative life.* Mahwah, NJ: Paulist Press.

Lortie, D. (1975). *Schoolteacher.* Chicago: University of Chicago Press.

MacIntyre, A. (1981). *After virtue.* South Bend, IN: University of Notre Dame Press.

Manen, M. (1991). *Tact of teaching.* Albany, NY: SUNY Press.

Marble, M. (2003). *The great wells of democracy. The meaning of race in American life.* Cambridge, MA: BasicCivitas Books.

Martin, J. (2012). *The Jesuit guide to (almost) everything.* New York: Harper.

Martinez, M. R., & McGrath, D. (2014). *Deeper learning.* New York: New Press.

Margonis, F. (2009). John Dewey's racialized visions of the student and classroom community. *Educational Theory, 59*(1), 17–39.

Matthews, G. (1996). *The philosophy of childhood.* Cambridge, MA: Harvard University Press.

Meier, D. (2002). *The power of their ideas.* Boston: Beacon Press. (Original work published 1995)

Mills, C. (2005). "Ideal theory" as ideology. *Hypatia, 20*(3), 165–184.

Mishra, P. (2017). *Age of anger.* New York: Farrar, Straus and Giroux.

Missett, T., & Foster, L. H. (2015). Searching for evidence-based practice. *Journal of Advanced Academics, 26*(2), 96–111.

Moll, L. C., Amanti, C., Neff, D., & Gonzalez, N. (1992). Funds of knowledge for teaching: Using a qualitative approach to connect homes and classrooms. *Theory into Practice, 31*(2), 132–141.

Morris, A. K., & Hiebert, J. (2011). Creating shared instructional products: An alternative approach to improving teaching. *Educational Researcher*, *40*(5), 5–14.

Muirhead, R., & Rosenblum, N. (2018). The new conspiracists. *Dissent.* Retrieved from: https://www.dissentmagazine.org/article/conspiracy -theories-politics-infowars-threat-democracy

Munby, H. (1989). Reflection-in-Action and Reflection-on-Action. *Education and Culture*, *9*(1), 31–41.

Murrell, P. C., Diez, M., Feiman-Nemser, S. & Schussler, D. L. (2010). *Teaching as a moral practice: Defining, developing, and assessing professional dispositions in teacher education.* Cambridge, MA: Harvard Education Press.

Nieto, S. (2009). *Language, culture and teaching: Critical perspectives* (2nd ed.). New York: Routledge.

Noddings, N. (2005). What does it mean to educate the whole child? *Educational Leadership*, *63*(1), 8–13.

Noguera, P. (2003). *City schools and the American dream.* New York: Teachers College Press.

Nussbaum, M. (2012). *The new religious intolerance: Overcoming the politics of fear in an anxious age.* Cambridge, MA: Harvard University Press.

Oakeshott, M. (2001). *The voice of liberal learning.* Indianapolis, IN: Liberty Fund.

O'Neill, O. (2014). *Acting on principal.* New York: Cambridge University Press.

Paley, V. (1993). *You can't say you can't play.* Cambridge, MA: Harvard University Press.

Paley, V. (2005). *A child's work.* Chicago: University Press of Chicago.

Pappas, G. (2008). *John Dewey's ethics.* Bloomington: Indiana University Press.

Perl, J. M., Griffiths, P. J., Evans, G. R., & Davis, C. (2009). Apology for quietism: A sotto voce symposium. *Common Knowledge*, *15*(1), 1–6.

Poirier, R. (1987). *The renewal of literature.* New York: Random House.

Poirier, R. (1992). *Poetry and pragmatism.* Cambridge, MA: Harvard University Press.

Pope, D. (2003). *Doing school.* New Haven, CT: Yale University Press.

Powell, A., Farrar, E., & and Cohen, D. (1985). *The shopping mall high school.* Boston: Houghton Mifflin.

Ravitch, D. (2010). *The death and life of the great American school system.* New York: Basic Books.

Ritchart, R. (2015). *Creating cultures of thinking.* San Francisco, CA: Jossey-Bass.

Rockefeller, S. (1991). *John Dewey: Religious faith and democratic humanism.* New York: Columbia University Press.

Rodgers, C. (2002). Defining reflection: Another look at John Dewey and reflective thinking. *Teachers College Record, 104*(4), 842–866.

Rodgers, C. & Raider-Roth, M. (2006). Presence in teaching. *Teachers and Teaching, 12*(3), 265–287.

Rorty, R. (1998). *Achieving our country.* Cambridge, MA: Harvard University Press.

Rud, A. G., & Garrison, J. (2010). Reverence and listening in teaching and leading. *Teachers College Record, 112*(11), 2777–2792.

Saito, N., & Standish, P. (2012). *Stanley Cavell and the education of grownups.* New York: Fordham University Press.

Santoro, D. (2011a). Good teaching in difficult times: Demoralization in the pursuit of good work. *American Journal of Education, 118*(1), 1–23.

Santoro, D. (2011b). Teaching's conscientious objectors. *Teachers College Record, 113*(12), 2670–2704.

Schoenbach, L. (2012). *Pragmatic modernism.* New York: Oxford University Press.

Setiya, K. (2014). The midlife crisis. *Philosophers' Imprint, 14*(31), 1–18.

Sherman, S. (2013). *Teacher preparation as an inspirational practice.* New York: Routledge.

Shklar, J. (1984). *Ordinary vices.* Cambridge, MA: Harvard University Press.

Shklar, J. (1989). The liberalism of fear. In N. L. Rosenblum (Ed.), *Liberalism and the moral life* (21–38). Cambridge, MA: Harvard University Press.

Shusterman, R. (2012). *Thinking through the body.* New York: Cambridge University Press.

Smith, D., Fisher, D., & Frey, N. (2015). *Better than carrots or sticks.* Alexandria, VA: ASCD.

Sockett, H. (2012). *Knowledge and virtue in teaching and learning.* New York: Routledge.

Stengel, B. (2001). Making use of the method of intelligence. *Educational Theory, 51*(1), 109–125.

Stitzlein, S. M. (2017). Growth, habits, and plasticity in education. In L. Waks & A. English (Eds.), *John Dewey's Democracy and Education: A centennial handbook.* New York: Cambridge.

Stilling, D. (2006). *Natureplay* [Motion Picture]. United States of America: Natureplay.

Stroud, S. (2011). *John Dewey and the artful life*. University Park, PA: Penn State University Press.

Subban, P. (2006). Differentiated instruction: A research basis. *Internation Education Journal, 7*(7), 935–947.

Tolstoy, L. (1997a). *Gospel in brief*. (I. Hapgood, Trans.). Lincoln, NE: University of Nebraska Press. (Original work published 1883)

Tolstoy, L. (1997b). *A calendar of wisdom*. (P. Sekirin, Trans.). New York: Scribner. (Original work published 1912)

Tomlinson, C. (2001). *How to differentiate instruction in mixed-ability classrooms* (2nd ed.). Alexandria, VA: ASCD.

Tovani, C. (2011). *So what do they really know?* Portland, ME: Stenhouse.

Tyack, D., & Cuban, L. (1995). *Tinkering toward utopia*. Cambridge, MA: Harvard University Press.

Villegas, A. M., & Lucas, T. (2002). Preparing culturally responsive teachers. *Journal of Teacher Education, 53*(1), 20–32.

Wagner, J. (2004). Fishing naked. *Young Children, 59*(5), 56–62.

Walser, R. (1999). *Jakob von Gunten* (C. Middleton, Trans.). New York: New York Review Books. (Original work published 1909)

Wampole, C. (2012). How to live without irony. *New York Times*. Retrieved from https://opinionator.blogs.nytimes.com/2012/11/17/how-to-live-without-irony/

Weil, S. (1970). *First and last notebooks*. New York: Oxford University Press.

Wiggins, G., & McTighe, J. (2005). *Understanding by design* (2nd ed.). Alexandria, VA: ASCD.

Windschitl, M., Thompson, J., Braaten, M. (2011). Ambitious pedagogy by novice teachers? Who benefits from tool-supported collaborative inquiry into practice and why. *Teachers College Record, 113*(7), 1311–1360.

Wiseman, F. (1968). *High school* [Motion picture]. United States of America: Zipporah.

Wiseman, F. (1994). *High school II* [Motion picture]. United States of America: Zipporah.

Wittgenstein, L. (1999). *Tractatus Logico-Philosophicus*. (D. F. Pears & B. F. McGuinness, Trans.). New York: Routledge. (Original work published 1921)

Wittrock, M. C. (1974). Learning as a generative process. *Educational Psychologist,* *11*(2), 87–95.

Wolf, S. (2012). *Meaning in life and why it matters.* Princeton, NJ: Princeton University Press.

Wolin, S., & Schaar, J. (1970). *The Berkeley rebellion and beyond.* New York: New York Review Books.

Wormeli, R. (2003). *Day one and beyond.* Portland, ME: Stenhouse.

Wormeli, R. (2006). *Fair isn't always equal.* Portland, ME: Stenhouse.

# Index